Brew Your Retirement

SAVOUR THE PAUSE

RAJAT MATHUR

notionpress.com
INDIA · SINGAPORE · MALAYSIA

ISBN
Paperback 979-8-90342-288-3
Hardcase 979-8-90362-889-6

Contents

About The Author

Rajat Mathur is the Founder of **Silver Spring**, India's first dedicated **non-financial retirement transition coaching practice**, helping individuals and organisations navigate life beyond work with purpose and humour.

A **former Managing Director at Morgan Stanley**, Rajat spent over three decades building teams, leading talent functions, and mentoring people across Asia. After guiding countless careers, he realised that one transition most people never prepare for is **retirement**.

Today, as a **Retirement Transition Coach**, he helps people reimagine this phase, not as an ending, but as a renewal. Through Silver Spring workshops and his signature *Retirement Index*, Rajat blends insight, empathy, and gentle wit to guide others in crafting their "second innings."

Brew Your Retirement is his first book on Retirement, a light, engaging, and deeply relatable reflection on the emotional side of retiring. With his trademark blend of humour and realism, Rajat reminds readers that retirement isn't about slowing down, it's about starting differently.

When he isn't writing or coaching, Rajat enjoys painting, hiking, golf, and discovering new coffee blends, preferably while planning his next story.

Acknowledgements

This book wouldn't have been possible without the people who stood by me through the reflection, confusion, and quiet comedy that come with one's own retirement transition.

To my **family, Sangeeta, Ioli**, and **Daivik** - thank you for being my anchor, my cheerleaders, and my safe space. For patiently bearing with me as I navigated the strange mix of freedom and uncertainty that retirement brings. For letting me test ideas (and moods) over endless cups of tea, and for giving me permission to share snippets of our life in these pages. You gave me the courage to tell the truth, the small, real stories that make this journey human.

To my **colleagues, teammates, and my larger work family**, thank you for giving me memories that became material, and experiences that shaped who I am. You created moments worth writing about, and friendships that have outlasted meeting invites and project codes. My years with you were among the best any professional could hope for, filled with laughter, purpose, and an occasional madness that made it all worthwhile.

To my **bosses and mentors**, who supported me with grace and generosity as I began to step into this new phase, your encouragement turned what could have been a difficult exit into a confident beginning.

To my **Silver Spring team**, who now keep me energised and inspired as we build this retirement transition practice together, a special thank you to **Jayeeta Bezbora**, my constant collaborator, sounding board, and co-architect of this journey.

To my **friends**, who spent countless hours over coffee helping me reflect, refine, and eventually write, thank you for the caffeine, the laughter, and the clarity that came with both.

And to my **extended family**, for always being there with warmth, humour, and unwavering support, you've been my circle of calm through every change.

This book may have my name on the cover, but it carries a little bit of each of you in every line. Thank you for being part of my story and this coffee break.

Opening Ramble: Setting The Stage

Every book needs a doorway. This one opens not with theory or formulas, but with moments.

Why? Because retirement isn't a single event. It's not a date stamped on a letter, or the ceremonial cutting of a farewell cake. It's a journey made up of fragments: a conversation here, a reflection there, an unexpected laugh, a nagging doubt, a sudden clarity.

That's why I chose to write this book as 100 timestamps. Not chapters, not lessons but timestamps. Each one is a snapshot of thought, memory, or humour along the winding road of retirement. Together, they don't tell *the* story of retirement, but they may help you recognise *your* story within them.

Why 100?

Because retirement is too big for a single perspective. It stretches across a spectrum of emotions ranging from pride, fear, relief, boredom, curiosity to, not surprisingly, a lot of joy. Each timestamp is short enough to capture one specific shade of an emotion, but when stitched together, they form a fuller picture of the entire experience.

Think of the 100 timestamps as dots. On their own, they're small, almost ordinary, easy (and even tempting) to ignore. But connect them, and a pattern emerges: the arc of leaving behind a structured identity and stepping into a freer, messier but mostly richer one.

What You Will (and Won't) Find Here

This isn't a manual on financial planning. It won't tell you where to invest, when to withdraw, or how to calculate compound interest. Plenty of experts do that better than I ever could. And I am hoping you have consulted one who has helped you figure out the financial threshold that you need to cross.

What you *will* find is the non-financial side of retirement, the one less talked about, but just as critical. You'll find reflections on identity, purpose, routines, relationships, health, and humour. You'll see how small moments like deleting your work email app, or being asked if you want a senior discount carry surprising weight.

You'll also find humour woven in, because retirement, like life, is best faced with a smile.

How to Read This Book

You don't need to read in order. Each timestamp stands alone, like a page from a diary. You can dip in and out, read one a day, or binge ten in a sitting. Some will resonate immediately; others may lie quietly until a future moment makes them ring true.

Read it like you'd listen to an old friend, not for instructions, but for companionship.

A Word on Tone

Retirement can feel daunting. But it doesn't have to feel heavy. Yes, there are serious questions to wrestle with: Who am I without my title? How do I fill my days? What do I want to leave behind?

But there are also moments of comic relief. Like realising you've become the family's default IT support. Or discovering that naps, once considered guilty indulgences are now celebrated lifestyle choices.

This book honours both sides: the reflection and the ridiculous. Because retirement is never just one or the other.

What I Hope You Take Away

If nothing else, I hope these 100 timestamps remind you that retirement is not an end state. It's not a retreat. It's a rewiring.

You may not find all your answers here but you may find better questions. And perhaps, reassurance that the doubts and laughter, the stumbles and small triumphs, are all part of the same human process.

So whether you are five years away, already in it, or just curious, welcome. Dip into these pages, take what resonates, leave what doesn't. Let the timestamps nudge you, amuse you, maybe even challenge you.

And as you turn to the first one, remember: this isn't a rulebook. It's a mirror. Sometimes foggy, sometimes funny, but always reflecting the journey we're all bound to take in our own time, in our own way.

This is about your new Spring.

Phase 1

The Whisper

Moments when the idea of retirement starts to form

What is Phase 1?

This phase is the quiet beginning, the part no one announces on LinkedIn.

It starts as a whisper: a meeting you don't want to attend, a Monday that arrives heavier than usual, a holiday where you feel more alive than at work.

You're not "quitting." You're noticing. Your energy is shifting from adrenaline to alignment. Expect internal arguments: Am I being ungrateful? Is this a phase? What if I regret it?

Rather than fight the voice, give it structure.

Capture three lists: (1) What energises me now? (2) What drains me reliably? (3) What I'd explore with zero consequence. Have one adult conversation at home, not to decide, but to surface hopes and fears on both sides.

Treat this period like due diligence on your own life: observe patterns, don't prosecute them. The goal of Phase 1 is not action; it's awareness. When you can say, "I'm curious about a different rhythm and I'm willing to test it," you're ready to move on.

You are not leaving something; you are moving toward something you can't fully name yet. That's okay. Curiosity is the runway light.

Timestamp #01: The First Whisper: "Should I Retire?"

It didn't arrive with thunder. No resignation letters drafted in frustration. No dramatic "I quit" moments. Just a whisper that is quiet enough to sometimes miss if I hadn't been paying attention. I was halfway through a meeting, the kind where slides recycled themselves and discussions circled endlessly, when the thought tiptoed in: "Maybe it's time to retire." Completely out of the blue. No Warning.

Not today. Not tomorrow. But someday. The whisper lodged itself in my mind like a song on repeat. At first, I brushed it off. Fatigue, surely. Or envy, after all, a friend had just sent photos from a post-retirement trek, looking annoyingly radiant. But the whisper didn't leave.

What struck me most wasn't fear. It was a sense of curiosity. What would life look like if it wasn't carved into meetings and deadlines? Would I finally paint again? Or spend mornings on golf courses rather than in boardrooms? The whisper wasn't pushing me out. It was pulling me forward.

And of course, with curiosity came doubt. Who am I without a title? Would I miss the rush? Or worse, would no one miss *me*? But here's the thing: not every whisper needs an immediate answer. Some just want to be heard. And that's when retirement begins, not with a financial plan, but with the quiet honesty of admitting: *there might be more to me than this role I've played so well.*

Timestamp #02: The First Time You Say It Out Loud

It slipped out one evening, over dinner, without ceremony.

"I've been thinking about retiring."

Just like that. No plan. No timeline. Just five words that hung heavier than I expected.

My spouse looked up. Not alarmed, not dismissive. Just thoughtful. A pause, a nod, and a calm, "Are you ready?"

I wasn't. Not even close. But that didn't matter. The thought had now left the safety of my mind and entered the world. And once you let it out, you can't put it back.

That first conversation didn't resolve anything. It wasn't meant to. What it did was make the idea *real*. It's one thing to toy with thoughts in your head. It's another to hear them spoken aloud. There's vulnerability in that moment and an almost strange kind of relief.

The reactions vary. Some (and only some) friends nod in envy. Others (mostly) panic, as though you've announced you're moving to another planet, Mars would be my choice for now. But the truth is, you're not declaring the end of your relevance.

You're simply saying: *I'm open to a new chapter.* And often, the courage to start comes not from your detailed financial planning and analysis on spreadsheets or from the company HR policies on retirement, but from seven little words spoken over dinner.

Timestamp #03: Looking at the Calendar Differently

For years, my calendar was gospel. Back-to-back meetings, colour-coded like a Picasso painting. A blank space at 10 AM? Panic! Something must've been missed.

But after that first whispered thought of retirement, I began looking at the calendar differently.

I'd scan a recurring meeting and wonder: *What if I wasn't here for this?* Not in the "I'll call in sick" way. In the "I might not be working here next year" way. Slowly, each entry shifted from obligation to option.

That 5-year strategy offsite? I could skip it, hypothetically. That annual review cycle? Maybe do it one last time and then it's someone else's problem next time.

It became a game. Mentally cancelling events months in advance. Outlook, bless it, kept reminding me about "Focus Time." I almost expected it to pop up one day with, *"Hey Champ, why are you still here?"*

Humour aside, this subtle shift matters. Retirement doesn't begin with your last day at work. It begins the moment you stop treating your calendar as sacred.

When you realise those white spaces don't represent laziness, instead they represent freedom.

Timestamp #04: When Weekend Plans Start to Feel Like Practice

Saturday morning.

Tea. Newspaper. Walk/Run/Golf/Gym. Repeat.

At some point, I realised my weekends were starting to feel suspiciously like practice runs for retirement. Trial versions of a life without alarms or deadlines.

I'd linger a little longer over breakfast. Take the longer, more scenic route on my walk. Sit with a book, not because I had the time, but because I wanted to. And the oddest part? The guilt began to fade. I didn't feel unproductive. I felt human. I felt myself.

It's almost comical that you spend decades treating weekends as recovery time, compressed between the Friday exhaustion and sometimes relief and Monday blues, sometimes the dread.

Then one day, you catch yourself thinking: *I could do this full-time.*

That's when you know retirement isn't some distant finish line. It's already creeping into your weekends, slowly negotiating a lease on your Monday mornings. And the more you rehearse, the more you realise: you're not stepping into emptiness. You're stepping into a presence.

Timestamp #05: The Colleague Who Retired and What It Sparked in You

We all have that one colleague. The steady presence. The dependable one. The person who never made a fuss, who somehow became part of the office furniture, not in the background, but in a way that anchored everyone else. Meetings ran smoother because they were there. Projects got finished because they kept nudging them along. And the coffee machine seemed to work better when they were around.

Then one day, almost out of nowhere, they announce their retirement.

Not with a bang, not with drama. Just a polite email. Maybe a simple subject line: *"Moving On."* There's a farewell cake in the pantry, a few speeches, the obligatory photo with balloons and streamers. And then… gone. Just like that.

At first, you shrug it off. "Good for them," you tell yourself, while juggling the usual Monday madness. They deserve it. Thirty, forty years of service, they've earned their rest. But then, something strange happens.

It sneaks up on you later, maybe when you're stuck in traffic the next morning, or trapped in yet another "quick sync" that is neither quick nor a sync. You picture them at that exact moment. No alarms. No deadlines. No commute. No Teams notifications lighting up their phone. Just freedom. Just presence.

And you feel something you didn't expect: envy.

Not envy of their absence from work, though that's tempting, but envy of their presence in their own life. The luxury of deciding what to do with their morning, not what the calendar dictates. The gift of time without an agenda.

That's when retirement stops being an abstract concept. It's no longer something that happens to "other people," sometimes far away. It becomes immediate. Personal. Possible. Because if they can walk away, so can you. And if you're honest with yourself, deep down, you kind of want to.

Their farewell isn't just their ending. It's also marking your beginning. Not in a dramatic, "I'm done" way. But in a quiet seed-planting way. A shift in perspective that lingers. You start noticing weekends differently. You question why you sit in meetings that drain you. You wonder, for the first time in years, what life outside work might actually feel like.

And here's the most ironic part: they have no idea they've done this for you. While they're busy stepping into their new phase, they've triggered the first real thought of yours. Their departure is your whisper. Their ending is your nudge to begin.

Retirement is contagious like that. Sometimes it only takes one colleague, steady, dependable, quietly walking away to make you ask: *When is it my turn?*

Timestamp #06: Browsing Retirement Content at Midnight

Everyone has a guilty midnight habit. I don't stay awake that late most nights though. Mine used to be cricket highlights earlier, more recently Instagram reels while sneaking some ice cream scoops while the rest of the house gently snored.

Then it became… retirement blogs. Articles like "Top 10 Things to Do After You Retire." YouTube videos of people converting their cars into long drive cruisers (I am a sucker for holiday vans). Forums about volunteering, trekking, even pottery (once).

Midnight Rajat was a dreamer. Morning Rajat, of course, denied it ever happened.

But midnight is honest. It strips away titles and performance reviews. At that hour, you're not an executive or a consultant. You're just someone wondering: *What could life look like beyond the inbox?*

I'd laugh at some of the ideas. (Me? Sports Coach at a School? Really?) But others stuck. A baking class (even if it is with Mom), a long trek, maybe even writing again.

Slowly, these late-night scrolls became my quiet rehearsal for life after work. Not planning, exactly. More like imagining. And sometimes, imagining is the most important step before the real thing happens.

Timestamp #07: The Arithmetic of Retirement: Mentally Calculating "How Many Years Left?"

It starts as harmless arithmetic.

"If I stay till sixty, that's X years. But what if I go at fifty-eight? Could I go earlier?"

You pull out calendars, calculators, sometimes even Excel. Subtract annual holidays. Reduce the weekends. Don't forget public holidays. Should you include the work-from-home days, or are those honorary "non-days"? By the time you're done, you've reverse-engineered your life into neat boxes of working days remaining.

And then the arithmetic gets absurd. You look at your wardrobe and think, "I've got five formal trousers. That means each one only needs to last these many cycles before retirement." You're not just counting years anymore. You're measuring your future in trousers, ties, and cafeteria lunches.

But somewhere in that silliness, a shift happens. Add one more bonus cycle. Delay until after the next project. Suddenly, you're not asking *if* you'll retire. You're asking *when*.

It's a peculiar kind of maths. It has less to do with money and more to do with meaning. How many good years of energy do I have left? How many of those do I want to spend in boardrooms versus classrooms, golf courses, or mountains? The arithmetic stops being about survival. It becomes about choice.

The danger, of course, is that once you start calculating, it's hard to stop. You negotiate with yourself: "One more year." "Just until this phase of the project closes." "Let me hit this milestone first." But behind all those calculations lies a deeper truth: the clock has already started ticking in your head.

And honestly? That's liberating. For the first time, the timeline doesn't belong to your company, your boss, or the next project pipeline. It belongs to you.

What begins as numbers on a page ends as a quiet declaration. Retirement isn't a question of arithmetic at all. It's a question of alignment.

And when the maths starts whispering, you already know which way the balance tilts.

Timestamp #08: That Talk With your Partner: It's not a Solo Act

Retirement isn't a solo act. It's a duet. Which is why the time you bring it up at home feels less like a financial decision and more like the opening scene of a play.

I remember saying it casually again one evening, over dinner: *"I think I'm getting closer to retiring."*

The silence that followed wasn't awkward, but it wasn't empty either. It was loaded. My spouse looked at me, not shocked, but curious. "Have you thought this through?"

The truthful answer? Not really. But saying it out loud again shifted the air. A thought that had only existed in my head was suddenly sitting between us at the table. Formally. We had moved forward from the first time I brought it up. This was getting real.

That conversation didn't end with a decision. It ended with questions. What would our days look like? Would we travel? Would we get under each other's feet? (Almost certainly, yes.) What would happen to the rhythm of our life when one of us suddenly stopped moving to the beat of Monday meetings and Friday deadlines?

And that's when it hit me: this wasn't my retirement. It was ours.

We walked and we talked. Sometimes in circles, sometimes into new territory. She started to dream too. Of the things we could finally do now that we were empty nesters. The dream holidays we had always postponed. Lazy Sunday brunches without me glancing at my phone. More time with friends. More time with each other.

But woven into those dreams was a dose of realism and honesty. She was clear: I would need to be out of the house for at least part of the day, or we would drive each other up the wall. As much as she looked forward to more time together, she also valued her space. Retirement, she pointed out, wasn't about suffocating each other. It was about rediscovering balance.

I appreciated that honesty. Support, yes. But also apprehension. Because retirement doesn't just rewrite my routine. It rewrites *ours*. It reshuffles how mornings begin, how afternoons are spent, how evenings feel.

And strangely enough, that made the whole idea less scary. Because it reminded me that I wasn't walking into this new phase alone. Retirement wasn't a solo journey into the unknown. It was a duet, full of negotiation, humour, compromise, and new rhythms we would learn together.

Every great journey feels easier when you're not walking it alone. And this one, I realised, might even come with a soundtrack.

Timestamp #09: The Day You Realize Work Doesn't Excite You Anymore

My ex-bosses may read this, so this one isn't easy to put out there. But here goes.

It wasn't a burnout. I wasn't angry. I wasn't running away. I was just... done.

I still remember the moment clearly. I was sitting in yet another meeting, one I had attended countless times before. Halfway through, it struck me that I already knew exactly how the conversation would unfold. The arguments, the counterpoints, the inevitable conclusion, it was all familiar. Nothing new. Nothing inspiring. Just another loop on the corporate carousel.

For the first time, I didn't feel guilty about letting my mind drift. Instead, a calm thought surfaced: *Maybe I've given all I have to give here.*

It wasn't depressing. It was clarifying. Work that once lit a fire inside me now barely sparked. That's when you know that it's not about quitting. It's about making space for something new to grow.

The frequency of that feeling began to intensify. At first occasional, then more persistent, until it became impossible to ignore. Almost distracting. I finally shared it with my boss, and to his credit, he understood. He appreciated the honesty.

Even then, you soldier on. You keep doing the work. You continue to prepare, to lead meetings, to deliver what's expected. You fight the creeping sense of detachment because you want to walk away the right way, head held high, proud of the journey. So you still give your best. You still show up. But each day, it gets a little harder to silence that voice reminding you it may be time.

What helped was being transparent. I wasn't retiring from life; I was retiring from the daily grind. There's a difference. This wasn't about fading away; it was about redefining what meaningful work looked like for me. I had begun quietly planning my next crusade, one that felt more personal and purposeful.

Not just golf lessons, though heaven knows I desperately needed those. It was about shaping a new chapter around teaching, mentoring, creating, building something that mattered to me and to others.

Stepping away wasn't an escape. It was an arrival. An arrival at a place where I could finally say, with clarity and without regret: *I've given my all here. Now it's time to do something new.*

Timestamp #10: Feeling Guilt About "Wanting Out"

Here's the tricky part. The guilt.

You've had a good run. Great colleagues, meaningful work, the kind of career that people nod approvingly at in LinkedIn updates. So why on earth would you want to leave? The voice in your head whispers: *Ungrateful.*

That's the thing about guilt, it's sneaky. It dresses itself up as loyalty. It convinces you that staying too long is noble, even heroic. "Look at me," guilt says, "I'm still in the office when everyone else has moved on to better things, surely that's commitment!" In reality, it's just inertia wearing a suit. Staying isn't always the braver option; sometimes it's just the easier one.

Retirement isn't about abandoning ship. You're not deserting the crew in the middle of a storm. You've done your time steering the vessel, patching leaks, and occasionally bailing out water with a teacup. You've built, you've led, you've given. Now, maybe it's time to give differently to a different field, a different set of individuals, in a very different environment.

A long-retired boss once nailed it when she said: "Retirement guilt is like survivor's guilt, except your colleagues are still in meetings." Brutal, but accurate. Because wanting out doesn't mean you've stopped caring. It means you're ready to care about new things. And that shift doesn't signal weakness, instead it signals wisdom. Hopefully.

Of course, guilt has other tricks. It whispers, "You'll miss this," usually right after a painfully long town hall or while fighting with the printer for the fifth time that day. (Spoiler: I don't miss the printer in my room.)

But you still show up, still give your best, because you want to leave with your head held high, not quietly sneaking out like someone dodging the office birthday cake celebrations.

The real truth? Guilt fades the moment you realise you're not retiring from *life* and that you're just retiring from *this* life. You're swapping recurring calendar invites for new pursuits, trading quarterly targets for personal milestones, and replacing performance reviews with golf swings, hikes, or mentoring conversations.

So yes, guilt is real. But once you see it for what it is, just another meeting you don't need to attend then you're free to walk away with gratitude, humour, and hopefully a better golf handicap

Phase 2

Planting the Seed

You begin to explore and prepare

What is Phase 2?

Now curiosity needs a calendar. The runway is practical and emotional: you align dates, stakeholders, and expectations at work and at home.

You'll feel a tug to justify the decision with grand plans; resist. Replace "What's your next big thing?" with "What's my next right step?"

Map a two-year non-financial plan across four buckets: Body (movement, sleep, check-ups), Mind (learning, hobbies), People (family rhythms, adult friendships beyond work), and Purpose (ways to be useful, paid or not).

At work, start leaving breadcrumbs: document processes, share context, elevate others. At home, agree "house rules" for shared space and alone time. Create a micro-pilot: try a class, mentor one person, volunteer twice.

You're testing identity beyond a title. Expect oscillation, one day, you're sure; the next, you question everything. Normal. Anchor with rituals: morning walks, weekly reflections, one "no work talk" dinner.

The goal of Phase 2 is clarity with kindness: make a clean decision without burning bridges or romanticising either past or future. When preparation feels more relieving than scary, the exit timeline is real.

Timestamp #11: Reading Retirement as a Life Phase, not a Deadline

For years, retirement was a date. A line on my financial planning chart. A milestone circled in red, right after "kids' college" and just before "dream vacation." But one day, I stumbled across a video that described retirement as a *phase*, not a finish line.

That was the first time I stopped seeing it as an ending and started viewing it as a chapter. It's not about "retiring from". It's about "retiring into."

The idea made me laugh a little. Imagine introducing yourself at a party: "Hi, I'm Rajat. I'm in Phase Two." Sounds more like an Addiction recovery program stage. But there's truth in it. A phase is active, evolving, something you *live in*. A deadline, on the other hand, sounds like something you survive.

When I reframed it as a phase, I noticed I became more curious. Instead of asking, "When can I retire?" I started asking, "What do I want this phase to look like?" That's a much more energising question. Suddenly, I wasn't staring at a date. I was staring at possibilities.

And to be honest, that feels much better than staring at a calendar reminder that says "Final Day at Work."

Timestamp #12: Making a List of "Things I'll Finally Do"

Everyone makes this list. Admit it. The "When I Retire" list. Mine, I confess, was embarrassingly ambitious and unnecessarily long.

At the top sat the classics: *learn a musical instrument (I love the drums)*, an odd choice for someone who can't hold a tune. *Play golf like Tiger Woods* even though given how often my ball disappears into woods and water hazards, this may be more prophecy than goal.

Somewhere in the middle: *write another book* (which, technically, might be cheating since I'm already halfway there). And, of course, the Everest of domestic ambitions: *finally organise the papers and documents.*

The funny thing about this list is how it so easily mixes the profound with the absurd. *Rediscover my purpose* sits neatly beside *binge-watch all of Breaking Bad.*

Traveling the world somehow coexists with *learning how to make sourdough bread.*

The list isn't really about achievement at all. It's about permission. Permission to imagine life outside performance reviews, PowerPoints, and quarterly reports. Permission to dream, without having to explain yourself in a business case.

Of course, reality quickly humbles you. Half the list is pure fantasy. Spoiler: you're probably not going to become Ringo Starr. And your golf swing is unlikely to morph into Tiger's, no matter how many "retirement lessons" you sign up for. But that's not the point. The point is that the act of making the list itself is liberating.

When you put pen to paper, you're quietly saying: *I believe there will be time for me again.* That life won't always be dictated by alarms, calendars, and inboxes. That, eventually, you'll get to choose how you spend your hours.

Whether you tick everything off or not, you've already won. Because retirement isn't a contest, and the bucket list isn't a scoreboard. The making of the list is step one, it is a declaration that your imagination is still alive and well. Even if Kilimanjaro remains unclimbed and the paperwork never gets organised, the very fact you gave yourself permission to dream is the achievement.

Timestamp #13: Rewriting Your Financial Comfort Zone

Here's where the humour collides with reality. Everyone insists that retirement is about money. Advisors talk about portfolio returns, compounding charts, and withdrawal ratios. And yes, finances matter because you don't want your post-work life turning into a never-ending episode of "Survivor." But when I sat down with my planner, what struck me wasn't the spreadsheets or the percentages. It was the mental gymnastics that came with it.

"Do I really need three streaming subscriptions?" "Can I legitimately file golf memberships under 'wellness' expenses?" "Will my kids even want my oddball collection of unique cups, or will they simply upload it all on a reseller site?" These are not the questions you'll find in any retirement handbook, but they pop up anyway. And suddenly, you realise that financial comfort is less about the actual numbers and more about the psychology of spending.

It's not about whether you can afford something but it's about whether you can buy it without guilt. True retirement wealth is being able to order that overpriced cappuccino and not feel like you've just raided your emergency fund. It's shifting from "earning" to "enjoying." It's the subtle but significant transition from chasing a payslip to designing a life.

The surprising bit? You don't need absolute certainty. You don't need to predict the market, your medical expenses, or the exact date your knees will finally refuse to cooperate. What you need is enough confidence to say, "I can afford to try." Money may build the runway, but courage is what actually gets you airborne. Without that leap, the best-built plan just sits there, grounded.

And then there's this other mental trap: doing it all "for the kids." That noble refrain of self-sacrifice. But why, I ask? You've given them a solid education, a decent launchpad, maybe even tucked away some investments in their names. That's more than enough. At some point, you need to let them build their own world. Otherwise, you'll never get them off your payroll, and you'll still be paying for their phone plans when you're 70. Independence, after all, is not just a gift you give yourself and it's one you give them too.

The hard truth is this: your kids are not entitled to your retirement savings. They may inherit what's left, but that's a bonus, not a right. And honestly, most of them would rather inherit your stories, your health, and your laughter than a stressed-out parent who scrimped and saved just to pass down a larger balance.

So here's the unglamorous, liberating conclusion: the money is for you. For your cappuccinos, your quirky hobbies, your ill-advised golf swings, and yes, even your three streaming subscriptions. Retirement isn't about hoarding for others, instead it's about finally spending on yourself without apology. Because after decades of working for everyone else, you've earned the right to let your money work for you.

Timestamp #14: Talking to a Mentor Who Already Retired

There's nothing quite like talking to someone who has already stepped through the very door you're hesitating at. I remember sitting down for coffee with a mentor, a man who had retired five years earlier. I was ready for clichés about leisurely travel, lazy afternoons of golf, and the joy of chasing grandchildren around the house. Instead, he leaned in and said, "No one prepares you for how long the days can be if you don't have a plan."

Then, with a mischievous smile, he added, "And for heaven's sake, don't take up gardening unless you actually like plants. I lost most of the plants on the balcony before I figured that out." The lesson was clear: retirement without intention can feel less like freedom and more like a long stretch of unstructured hours.

That conversation has stayed with me. Over the years, in coaching others through their own transitions, I've seen versions of this truth play out again and again. One woman I coached had always dreamt of teaching. She thrived while conducting two-hour masterclasses. The applause, the energy, the exchange of ideas, all of it made her glow. But when she signed up for a regular teaching role, the shine faded quickly. The endless course preparation, assignments to grade, and student queries flooding her evenings was not the retirement she had imagined. It wasn't that she didn't love teaching. It was that she hadn't tested the full reality of it.

Another story came from a former CXO who joined a non-profit, hoping to use his skills for social good. Noble idea, great cause, meaningful work. But there was one tiny wrinkle. The organisation wasn't exactly flush with funds. That meant no business class, more economy, and on certain occasions, horror of horrors, the train. It sounds trivial until you realise how tightly our identities can be woven with our old perks. For him, this wasn't just about a seat on a plane; it was a daily reminder that his status had shifted. The proverbial straw that broke the camels back turned out to be a train ticket.

These stories highlight an uncomfortable but important truth: retirement is not about filling time; it's about shaping it. Time, left unstructured, stretches into an endless blur. Time, given intention, becomes rich, purposeful, and deeply satisfying. My mentor's advice echoes in my mind: experiment before you retire. Don't just assume travel, volunteering, or teaching will fit. Try them. Test them. Experience the full picture, not just the highlight reel.

I often tell people to think of it like marathon training. You wouldn't run 42 kilometres on a whim; you'd build stamina mile by mile. Give yourself a couple of years of runway. Use that time to explore hobbies, dabble in part-time commitments, and discover what energises you versus what drains you. Practice, push, recalibrate. That way, when the moment comes, you're not staring at endless empty days, but stepping into a rhythm you've already rehearsed. Retirement isn't the end of structure. It's the start of choosing your own.

Timestamp #15: The Retirement-Eligible Birthday

There's something sobering about the later-year birthday, the one that makes you "officially" eligible in your own head, even if HR policies still have a few years left on the clock.

It could be fifty, fifty-five, fifty-eight, or sixty. The number doesn't matter as much as the weight of the candle. That birthday feels heavier than the rest. You cut the cake, pose for photos, smile at the jokes, but inside you're running calculations. *If I walked away now, how many years would I really have to chase those dreams I've kept on hold?*

And strangely, it's not depressing. It's clarifying. These birthdays stop being about presents and start being about presence. They're not about gadgets, ties, or cakes anymore. They're about asking: *What do I want to be present for? Whose lives do I want to show up in?*

That's the real gift of these milestone years. They give you permission to take the idea of retirement seriously and not as a vague future event, but as a concrete possibility. They make you realise retirement isn't just about leaving something behind. It's about stepping into something else, something you design on your own terms.

When someone teased me on my birthday, "You're close to retirement age now!" I smiled and replied, *"Yes, and soon I'll finally qualify for discounted flight fares."* The joke landed, but beneath it was the truth: milestones matter, not because they limit us, but because they nudge us into honesty.

So yes, that later birthday changes things. It's less about the number of candles and more about what they illuminate. They light up a question we've all quietly rehearsed: *If not now, when?*

Timestamp #16: Looking at Your Work Legacy

There's a moment in everyone's career when you start to quietly wonder what will be left behind when you're not around anymore. Not morbidly, not in a gloomy way but just practically. What will linger after the farewell party, after the final email, after your name disappears from the org chart?

Will people really remember the big projects? The late-night calls? The carefully crafted speeches (or the impromptu ones)? Probably not. What they'll remember is how you made them feel.

I once asked a junior colleague what she'd remember most if I left. She paused, thought for a moment, and then said: *"That time you told me to take a holiday before the baby was born."* That was it. Not the strategy decks, not the recruitment metrics, not the KPIs I had agonised over. A simple piece of advice.

That's when it hit me: legacy isn't the title on your LinkedIn profile. It isn't the bullet points on your CV. It's the stories others tell about you when you're not in the room.

Sometimes it's the big moments, standing up for a team under pressure, guiding a course correction at the right time. More often, it's the small gestures. Lending an ear when someone needed to vent. Offering a gentle nod across a crowded meeting room that said, "You've got this." Sharing in someone's sorrows. Celebrating their small victories. Cracking a joke that diffused tension. These are the tiny threads that, woven together, form the fabric of memory..

And you don't get to decide your legacy. Others do. They will curate the stories, they will decide what's worth retelling. But you do have influence. Every interaction plants a seed. Every kindness, every bit of humour, every moment of patience adds to the garden you'll eventually leave behind.

Maybe the best retirement preparation isn't just financial planning or hobby-hunting. Maybe it's this: making sure the stories you leave behind are the kind you'd want to be remembered by.

Because when the titles fade and the metrics are forgotten, the stories will remain. And they will outlast everything else.

Timestamp #17: When the Torch Quietly Passes

One day, you realise you're no longer the one leading the conversation. The younger folks are. They're faster with the tools, sharper with the trends, and can fire off memes before you've even figured out how to react to the last one. You smile, nod, contribute when needed, but somewhere inside you know the torch has already been passed. You're not steering anymore; you're marking time.

The signs creep in subtly. You don't understand the lingo in meetings. Acronyms sound like secret codes. Someone mentions a platform and you're still not sure whether it's an app, a band, or a new kind of sneaker. You try to keep pace, but it's like chasing a tail you'll never catch. The world moves at breakneck speed while you're still knotting your ties perfectly and polishing your shoes every morning, convinced that neat laces somehow still matter.

At first, it stings. There's pride in being the one with the answers, the guide others turn to. Losing that feels like losing ground. But slowly, something shifts. You realise it's not about clinging to the centre anymore. It's about creating space for others to step forward. And when you do that, you discover a strange relief.

Because the truth is, it's no longer your job to master every new app, tool, or buzzword. It's your job to ask better questions, to mentor, to steady the ship when turbulence hits. And if you can laugh at yourself along the way, "No, I don't know what that app does, but I do know how to have a difficult conversation" then you retire not just with dignity, but with humour intact.

The torch always passes. The real legacy is how gracefully you let it go.

Timestamp #18: Discussing It with Family (and Their Reactions)

Families don't always react the way you expect. When I first brought up retirement at home, I braced myself to worry about conversations about finances, purpose, or health. Instead, my son grinned and said, *"Great, maybe you'll finally learn to be better at golf."* Not quite the deep discussion I had in mind, but honest nonetheless.

My spouse, on the other hand, was still weighing the possibilities of more time together, more travel, more brunch dates… but also the practical question of how to stay out of each other's way. Every family member saw retirement through their own lens.

And that's the thing: retirement doesn't just happen to the retiree. It ripples outward. For some, it feels like relief. For others, it looks like disruption. The trick, I realised, is to listen without getting defensive. Because when they react, they're not just reacting to *your* retirement. They're reacting to the ways it will reshape *their* lives too.

Eventually, we found humour in the conversation. Someone suggested a family trip. I countered with something smaller: maybe I'd just start by cooking dinner without burning it. Small wins first.

Of course, parents bring their own colour to the mix. My dad thinks it's too early, not because he doubts me, but because he still enjoys telling his friends my designation and then trying to guess my salary. For him, retirement means losing bragging rights. Indian moms are the same across households: my mother wasn't worried about me at all. She was worried for my wife. *"How will she manage you at home all day?"* she asked, with the knowing look of someone who has seen this before.

And then there's my daughter. She just laughed and said, *"You can't sit still for one minute. Retirement won't change that."* She might be right.

In the end, the whole conversation felt less like a family council and more like a family comedy. But maybe that's the point. Retirement planning doesn't begin in offices, or with calculators. It begins at home, around the dinner table, with jokes, worries, and dreams, all tangled together. And if you can laugh through it, you've already made the first step easier.

Timestamp #19: Creating a "Life After" Folder

On my computer, tucked away between work files and power point presentations, was a folder simply titled *"Life After."*

Inside? A jumble of random notes. Links to articles. A half-baked bucket list. Even a photo of a mountain trail I once dreamt of hiking. It looked more like a teenager's scrapbook than a grown-up plan. But it gave me comfort.

Every time work felt overwhelming, I'd sneak into that folder as if it were a guilty pleasure. In those moments, it reminded me that I was more than my job title, more than the inbox. My imagination had already begun building a bridge to what came next.

That the folder was never really about "planning." It was about hope. A quiet message to myself: *You have a future beyond work schedules and PowerPoints.* Sometimes, that reminder was all I needed to keep going.

Over the years, it went through more edits than any presentation I've ever done. Whenever I stumbled across something interesting, a hobby someone had taken up, a story of what another retiree had done, it got added to the list. A few weeks later, maybe it stayed, maybe it got scratched. But the act of collecting ideas was fun in itself. That's how my dabbling in painting began, it started as a line on the list and eventually became part of who I am.

At one point, I even printed the list. It lived on my desk at home, like a vision board disguised as a to-do list. Every so often, I'd revise it, reprint it, and replace the old one. For a while, I tried colour-coding it with green for non-negotiables, yellow for "maybe someday." It looked beautiful until I realised updating it every time meant starting from scratch with a printer and highlighters. The coding experiment didn't last long, but the spirit of the list did.

Looking back, that *Life After* folder was never about organisation. It was about imagination. About giving myself permission to believe there was life after the emails, the meetings, and the titles. And in its own messy, colourful way, it was proof that the future had already begun.

Timestamp #20: Worrying About Health (and Insurance)

Nothing says "you're getting older" quite like suddenly caring about insurance fine print. I used to skip those pages without a second glance. Now, I read them with the intensity of a thriller novel. The villain? Exclusions.

The truth is, one of the invisible perks of corporate life is the umbrella of health coverage. You don't think about it much while you're working. But the day you retire, that safety net shrinks. Suddenly, it's not just about planning for leisure or budgeting for travel. It's about realising you'll need to fend for yourself and your family's health will be one of the biggest line items.

A friend once joked, *"Your body at sixty is just a high-maintenance subscription. Cancel at your own risk."* Funny, yes, but also painfully accurate. Retirement planning isn't just about time and money. It's about making sure you're fit enough to enjoy the freedom you've worked for. Because what good is having all the time in the world if your body refuses to come along for the ride?

This isn't pessimism. It's biology. We are going to get older. We are going to creak, ache, and occasionally grunt when getting out of chairs. Doctor visits become more frequent. Diet plans start to look less like Instagram fads and more like lifelines. Yoga classes reveal muscles you didn't know existed and remind you they can still ache.

And yet, here's the upside: investing in your health is the only retirement strategy guaranteed to pay dividends. Unlike the markets, it doesn't depend on global sentiment or quarterly earnings. If anything, it appreciates with consistent effort. A good night's sleep, a regular walk, a decent diet, an occasional stretch, these add quietly, steadily, to your future balance sheet.

Best of all, health doesn't punish you for taking a nap. In fact, it rewards you. Every small act, from a morning jog to skipping that extra plate of fried food is a deposit into a fund that will matter far more than your retirals

So yes, study the fine print. Learn the exclusions. But remember: the real policy is the one you write with your own habits

Phase 3

The Emotional Rollercoaster

The months leading up to retirement

What is Phase 3?

Welcome to the emotional whiplash: nostalgia on Tuesday, impatience on Wednesday, panic on Thursday. You're grieving a season while still living in it. That paradox can feel strange, like packing for a move while hosting a party.

Name the feelings without editing them: pride, loss, relief, guilt. All true. This is also the time to audit identity hooks: email signature, corner seat, the dopamine of being "needed." Notice where your worth has entangled with status.

Begin gentle untangling: say no to being the default firefighter; say yes to mentoring others to handle it. Practically, start lightening the backpack, declutter drawers, files, and mental tabs. Capture "institutional memory" you want to give forward.

Expect well-meaning advice and a few sideways comments. Receive the love, ignore the noise. At home, rehearse new rhythms: a half-day out of the house; shared calendars for alone and together time.

The aim here is emotional readiness, not perfection. If you can tell a simple, honest exit story, "It's time for my next season; I'm grateful for this one".

You've stabilised enough to enter the final stretch.

Timestamp #21: The Retirement Letter You Don't Send Yet

It starts as a draft. Subject line: *"Retirement Announcement."* You type a few lines. Gratitude, nostalgia, maybe even a half-joke about finally dusting off the golf clubs. Then you pause. You're not ready. So you save it quietly in Drafts, like a secret you're not yet prepared to share.

I wrote mine years before I ever pressed send. Not months but years. It went through countless iterations. Some versions read like epic speeches. Others were short and sharp, barely more than a paragraph. By the time the real day came, I must have been on version forty-seven. Each one felt final at the time, until it didn't.

The unsent letter changes you. Just knowing it exists alters the way you show up. You walk into Monday meetings differently. You're no longer desperate to prove yourself, no longer clinging to every agenda point. Somewhere inside, you've already whispered goodbye, even if only to yourself.

That draft becomes a kind of safety valve. It reminds you that you could leave, that you're not trapped. It's proof that staying is still a choice and that choice is powerful.

Over time, the letter evolves from a practical announcement into something more symbolic. It becomes a mirror. It reflects your shifting priorities, your quiet hopes, your growing readiness. Some days you read it and think, *not yet*. Other days, you hover over the send button and feel the pull of freedom just one click away.

Eventually, of course, there will be a day when you hit send. The inboxes will ping, the messages will pour in, and your secret draft will finally become public. But until that moment, the draft sits patiently, reminding you of a truth most people forget: retirement isn't a cliff you fall off. It's a door you prepare to open, in your own time, on your own terms.

And sometimes, even an unsent email is enough to change the way you live today.

Timestamp #22: Second Guessing the Decision

Retirement isn't a straight line. One day you're absolutely convinced it's time. The next, you're hunched over your laptop, secretly Googling *"Am I too young to retire?"* like a nervous teenager looking for permission.

Here's the truth: you will never be completely sure. Retirement is a decision, not a formula. And it's a big one, life changing, in fact. Not just for you, but for everyone around you. Your family, your colleagues, your team, even your boss. The ripples of your choice will reach further than you think.

Naturally, the doubts pile up. *What if I get bored? What if I'm not ready? What if I secretly love looking at humongous amounts of data and run Power BI reports?* (Spoiler: you don't.)

Second-guessing is normal. After all, you've spent decades moving to a rhythm, filling every slot in your calendar. Stepping away feels like stepping off a treadmill. It is scary, wobbly, and guaranteed to leave you clinging to the side rails for a while.

And that's where the temptation creeps in: "Just one more year." Stay a little longer. Close this project. Wait for that bonus. Then decide. But once you start down the "one more year" path, it rarely stops. Succumb once, and you'll find a hundred reasons to keep running in place. The treadmill never ends unless you choose to step off.

What makes stepping away so daunting is the empty calendar. The fear isn't just about money or title, it's about being unwanted, unloved, unoccupied. But retirement isn't about losing your schedule; it's about redesigning it. Filling it not with what others demand of you, but with what you choose for yourself.

The trick, I've learned, is to laugh at the doubts without letting them drive the decision. Retirement doesn't require 100% certainty. It only requires enough confidence to try.

Because once you step off the treadmill, shaky legs and all, you realise the ground underneath is solid and it's yours.

Timestamp #23: The Day You Realize Your Identity Is Tied to Your Email Signature

"XYZ, Managing Director."

There it is. Crisp font, bottom of every email. Your name, your identity, your instant credibility. A single line that opens doors, ends debates, and signals authority before you've even typed a word. For years, it's been as much a part of you as your actual name.

But one day, you look at it differently. You read it and think: *Who am I without this line?*

It's a sobering question. Because when you strip away the signature, the title, the corporate brand, you're left with... just you. And that feels unsettling at first. It stings the first time you imagine introducing yourself at a gathering without the safety net of a company name attached.

Try this experiment at home: introduce yourself without mentioning your designation or the organisation you work for. Just your name. That's it. Notice how naked it feels. Almost scary. Because in that moment, you realise how much of your identity has been tethered to a digital footer.

And yet, this is the very muscle retirement forces you to build. For every man or woman needs an identity, a way of answering the "So what do you do?" question that doesn't lean on the past. You can only ride "Former Managing Director" for so long before it starts sounding like an old trophy gathering dust.

This is the uncomfortable but necessary gain: learning to define yourself without reference to a corporate logo. To be someone whose worth doesn't shrink when the job title disappears.

One friend told me he solved it by replacing his old email signature with a new one: *"Professional Human Being."* I laughed, but also admired the honesty. But is that enough

Retirement, in that sense, isn't about losing your signature. It's about rewriting it.

Timestamp #24: When You Stop Fighting for Promotions

Once upon a time, every promotion felt like oxygen. You chased them with determination, celebrated them like milestones, and built your calendar around them. The announcement email, the congratulatory calls, even the updated LinkedIn headline, it all felt electric.

But somewhere along the way, something shifts. You realise you've stopped caring. The next rung on the ladder doesn't sparkle anymore. The title sounds impressive, sure, but the excitement doesn't land the same way.

This isn't defeat. It's perspective. You've climbed high enough to enjoy the view, and it's not bad at all. So you start asking harder questions: Do I really want to spend my remaining years in performance calibration meetings? Do I need more late-night calls, more stress, more "stretch targets"? Or would I rather invest that same energy in actually living?

Because promotions, by definition, mean a bigger job. More responsibility. More pressure. But never more time. The calendar doesn't expand to match the new title, instead it just gets tighter. Slowly, you begin to wonder: is this really the life I want to lead?

And that's when the truth begins to dawn. Designations, as shiny as they may be, are only temporary additives to your identity. They boost the flavour while you're in the game, but they dissolve the moment you step away. One day, no matter how high you've climbed, the title will fall away.

The charm of promotions fades when you realise you don't need another one to prove anything. You've already done enough. You've contributed, delivered, led, and built. Your worth doesn't rest on another announcement in the organization.

And maybe that's the quiet gift of perspective. You stop chasing the next rung and start appreciating the ground you're already standing on.

Timestamp #25: The Unexpected Sadness of "Lasts"

Retirement often comes wrapped in a long list of "lasts." The last budget cycle. The last town hall. The last time someone asks you to "just jump on a quick call."

You don't always notice them when they happen. You're too busy getting through the day. It's only later that the realisation sneaks in; *that was the last one.* And with it comes a quiet sadness. Not for the tasks themselves (let's be honest, nobody misses quarterly reviews), but for the familiarity. The rituals that shaped your days, the rhythms you could set your watch by.

Mark these moments with gratitude. Pour yourself a glass of wine after sending that final late-night email. Pause and smile after your last "all-hands" meeting, knowing you'll never again have to decipher a slide full of corporate jargon. Even the final Monday morning commute deserves recognition. Not because you'll miss the traffic, but because you survived it for decades.

Of course, the list of lasts can feel endless. The last appraisal season. The last working weekend. The last time your phone buzzed with "urgent, needed by EOD." But each last is also a quiet first. The first day you no longer need to log in. The first Monday you spend at a café instead of a cubicle.

Retirement isn't about mourning the list of lasts. It's about noticing them, honouring them, and then stepping forward into the freedom of "firsts."

Timestamp #26: Cleaning Out Drawers: Physical and Emotional

There's something strangely symbolic about that final desk clean-out. And it happens over a period of time.

At first, it feels practical, emptying drawers, boxing up files. But soon, it becomes more like a time capsule excavation.

You find pens that no longer work, folders dated more than a decade ago, and a drawer full of stress balls from forgotten offsites. Most of it heads straight to the bin, but every now and then you pause over a trinket; a coffee mug, a paperweight, a random corporate giveaway and realise you're not just decluttering your desk. You're decluttering a version of yourself.

The surprises come quickly. Cards you'd forgotten, small gifts from colleagues, long-ignored trophies. Shredding papers kept "just in case" and documents no one ever looked at twice but somehow survived for ten years. The act of deciding becomes its own ritual: one pile to throw away, one pile to take home (only to throw away later), and one small pile to keep. That "keep" box fills up far quicker than you'd expect.

Then there are the awkward items. Photo frames with team pictures, too meaningful to discard, but impossible to display at home. Post-it notes with cryptic reminders that make no sense anymore. Passwords written in shorthand you can no longer decode. And of course, the stress balls.

As you sift through it all, the physical clean-out begins to trigger an emotional one. You start letting go of more than clutter. Old grudges.

Minor regrets. The "should-haves" and "if onlys." The drawer becomes a mirror, reflecting not just the career you built, but the baggage you've been carrying. And with every folder shredded, every pen tossed, you feel a little lighter.

That's the hidden gift of retirement. It gives you permission to travel lighter, both literally and mentally. To decide what to carry forward and what to finally leave behind.

Though let's be honest, the stress balls always come home. They're far too useful for squeezing during cricket matches.

Timestamp #27: Farewell Lunches Start Getting Scheduled

There's an unspoken signal in every office. Once farewell lunches start showing up on your calendar, the countdown has begun. Suddenly, you're in demand like never before. Colleagues want "one last coffee," "one last lunch," or "just a quick catch-up." For a few weeks, you're more popular than the cafeteria's biryani.

It's flattering, no doubt. But also exhausting. Because retirement isn't just about you stepping away, it's about everyone else preparing to say goodbye to their version of you.

For some, it's the chance to squeeze in one last bit of free advice (yep, no invoice as yet). For others, it's sheer curiosity: *How did you decide it was time?* A few can't resist offering their unsolicited counsel: *You could stay longer, what's the hurry?* And then there are the emotional ones, who tear up even while reassuring you that social media will keep everyone "connected."

Most of these encounters, though, are genuine and heartfelt. People want to acknowledge the role you've played in their journey. And with nothing left to prove, you find yourself more open too, sharing words of wisdom without the weight of office politics or hierarchy. You start to feel like free-floating particles. Or worse, an atom untethered. (That part can be a little worrying.)

"Stay in touch." becomes the most repeated phrase in the room. Whether or not they do, you learn to accept the sentiment for what it is: a kind farewell, a bridge left open.

A word of practical advice: pace yourself. Don't schedule more than three farewell lunches in a week. Even retirement can't protect you from cholesterol. And yes, keep the coffees in check, for too many and you'll retire with a caffeine habit.

Timestamp #28: Sorting Memories from Achievements

When you look back, the achievements blur. The sessions, the deals, the deliverables, the quarterly numbers on the report, all part of a good run, but indistinct in hindsight. What stays clear are the memories.

The joke in the elevator that became office folklore. The road trip for an offsite, with stories that grew taller with every retelling, part fact, part generous exaggeration. The day your team surprised you with cake at 5 a.m. in the car park because they'd found out about your promotion before you did. Those are the moments that don't fade.

Sorting memories from achievements is humbling. Because you realise that people rarely remember the exact numbers you delivered. They remember how you made them feel. Retirement, in a way, lets you lean into that truth to measure life not by spreadsheets but by stories.

The small gestures matter more than the big wins. Offering advice at the right moment. Listening when someone needed an ear. Back then, they felt like tasks. Today, they stand out as memories.

And let's be honest: the stories are far more fun at dinner parties. They raise a glass to the pranks, the late-night laughs, and the moments of kindness that stitched a career together.

As for the trophies, that's always a dilemma. Should you leave them behind as relics of the office? Or take them with you as proof of battles won? I compromised and some I carried, some I left. Today, the ones I kept sit quietly in a cardboard box, no longer demanding shelf space.

Because in the end, the real trophies were never the ones engraved in metal. They were the stories etched into memory.

Timestamp #29: Upgrade to Observer Class

You're still in the room, technically. The chair has your imprint, your coffee mug is loyally parked next to your desktop, and yet... the conversation has floated around you. No one asked you to leave, but no one's exactly looking at you either for all the answers. You've become corporate wallpaper. Still pretty though.

At first, it bruises the ego. You feel the itch to jump in, to remind everyone that you still know a thing or two about "synergies" and "go-forward plans." But then it dawns on you: this isn't exile. It's a promotion. You've been quietly upgraded to *Observer Class.*

No deadlines. No deliverables. Just the luxury of sipping your tea while watching everyone else squirm under the weight of action items. Invisibility, it turns out, is strangely liberating.

You can doodle on notepads without guilt, tune out jargon with Olympic-level focus, you can cheer for the quick wins, but when the discussion shifts to three-year transformation projects, you smile and think, *please, I'll be on a beach by then.*

Unapologetic.

You set up the playbook. The systems will run, the processes will hum, and if they don't? Well, that's someone else who will step up and make it happen, not you, anymore.

Spectator mode becomes a rehearsal for retirement. You're practicing the art of stepping back without falling off the stage. And yes, it's a peculiar mix of a tiny heartbreak to realise the company can survive without you, but also a massive relief to know that it does.

So you lean back. Loosen the grip. Let them carry the torch. You've done your part.

The real thing? While they're sweating over the next quarterly target, you're quietly practicing for the bigger game: running *your* world. And in this new spectator sport, the season tickets are free, the snacks are better, and there's no boss demanding a "deck by Monday."

Now that, if you ask me, is the best exit strategy of all.

Timestamp #30: Counting Down in Private

Here's the secret no one tells you: long before HR formally knows, you start your own countdown. A quiet tally in your head. Maybe a number scribbled on a sticky note. In my case, it was a little figure in the corner of my whiteboard that I updated every few days like a secret code only I could read.

It was right there in front of me, a constant reminder. And far from being morbid, the countdown was energising. Every "last" meeting became easier when I knew the exact number of Mondays left. I smiled more. I sweated less. I stopped caring about the politics over who got the corner office because I was about to check out altogether.

That private countdown gave me power. The power of anticipation. The joy of a secret. The calm that comes from knowing you're almost free. While everyone else still raced to deadlines, I was quietly rehearsing my exit.

Of course, secrets don't stay secret for long. My assistant noticed it first. She'd been with me too long to miss something like that. "What's this number?" she asked one morning. I couldn't lie, so I told her. She promptly rubbed it off and said, "You're not going anywhere." She meant it kindly, but in this case, she was wrong.

After that, it became a running game. Every time I rewrote the number, she would come in later and scrub it off. Some days it stayed visible, some days it didn't, but the countdown never stopped. It lived quietly in my head, ticking down even when no one could see it.

Looking back, that little ritual wasn't just about leaving. It was about control. About having a small, private bridge between the life I had and the life I was walking into. Retirement can feel like a cliff, but a secret countdown turns it into steps, one number at a time.

Phase 4

The Exit Ramp

The transition intensifies

What is Phase 4?

This phase compresses a career into a handful of days: handovers, exit interviews, farewell messages, the last ID beep.

It's easy to perform gratitude and miss feeling it. Slow down. Write three notes: to a peer who made you better, to a junior you believe in, to someone invisible who kept the place running.

Handovers are not file dumps; they're context gifts, what to watch for, who to call, how not to break the thing.

Expect mixed theatre: speeches, cake, awkward jokes about golf. Let people love you in their idiom. Take photographs of ordinary places, the corridor light at 8 p.m., the view from your desk. Ritualise the final commute: walk a little slower, say a private thank-you.

At home, mark the transition with a small celebration that isn't about work, your people carried this decision too.

The goal of Phase 4 is closure without a hangover: you leave clean, proud, and light.

When your calendar clears and your body exhales rather than panics, you're ready for the "firsts."

Timestamp #31: The Day You Submit the Official Resignation

No confetti. No champagne corks. No Morgan Freeman narrating your life in the background. Just you, a tired laptop, and Outlook. A single cursor. A single button: *Submit.*

For a moment, you hesitate. Not because you're unsure, you've had this date etched in your head for months but because it feels absurdly small. After decades of corporate battles, all the late nights, the strategies, the budgets, the "quick updates" that lasted three hours… your entire career now hinges on one click. The big finale reduced to something even less dramatic than ordering groceries online.

Click.

That's it. No standing ovation.

While the world doesn't shift, something inside you does. A lightness creeps in. The invisible tether to performance cycles, appraisals, and org charts snaps. The thought occurs, deliciously that you will never again have to draft a self-assessment with "Exceeded Expectations" wedged in somewhere between your actual exhaustion and your manager's "let's keep it modest."

Of course, alongside relief comes a little ache. Not the kind that requires tissues, but a quiet pang. You've lived inside this machine so long that part of you wonders who you are outside it. It's like watching a long-running TV series end. You loved the characters, even the annoying ones, but you're also ready for the spinoff.

And then comes the smirk. The one you can't suppress. Because while everyone else is busy preparing slides for the next Monday meeting, you've just deleted Mondays from your life. That's right. Gone. Erased. Along with performance reviews, compliance training, and the mysterious "all hands" meetings where no hands were ever required.

You look at the screen one last time, almost expecting it to thank you for your service. It doesn't. But you? You're already free.

No soundtrack, no fireworks, just a blinking cursor and a future wide open.

And honestly, that's better. Fireworks fizzle. This? This is permanent.

Timestamp #32: The Exit Interview

The exit interview. That curious corporate rite of passage, where HR hands you a polite smile and a notepad (real or digital) and asks the immortal question: *"Do you have any feedback for the organisation?"*

Feedback? Where does one even start? After decades, you're tempted to roll out a scroll like a medieval town crier: "Hear ye, hear ye! Fewer meetings, stronger coffee, and for heaven's sake, stop calling this a family. Families don't send you three reminder emails about completing your mandatory training before the deadline."

But really, they were family; you spent time with them.

But then you remember: subtlety is an art. Too safe, and you sound bland. Too savage, and your name goes down in folklore as "that bitter retiree who torched the bridge while walking off it." The sweet spot lies somewhere between constructive suggestion and well-timed stand-up comedy.

Because retirement gives you superpowers. You no longer need to play politics, protect your promotion chances, or phrase every complaint as a "development opportunity." You can actually say what you mean and with a smile. And oddly enough, people listen more when they sense you have nothing left to gain.

So you try the middle path. Yes, fewer meetings would help productivity. Yes, maybe improve the coffee. And yes, perhaps don't call people "resources" when they are, inconveniently, actual humans. You drop in a joke about conference calls that could've been short one line e-mail messages, and the HR rep chuckles while still scribbling notes.

And when it ends, you realise something. The exit interview isn't really for you. It's for them, the ones still running the race. You're just the runner stepping off the track, tossing a few pointers to those still gasping for breath.

You shake hands, leave the room, and think: *That's the last "interview" of my life.* No prep, no panel, no post-mortem email. Just the clean break of walking out with the freedom to finally give unfiltered answers to life's next questions.

Timestamp #33: Goodbye With the Team (And the Ones Who Surprised You)

The farewell isn't really about who shows up. It's about who surprises you by showing up. That quiet analyst you barely remembered mentoring who suddenly thanks you for advice you gave in a corridor ten years ago. The intern who nervously admits you inspired them to stay in the profession. Those little moments knock you sideways, because you realise your impact was invisible to you, but clearly not to them.

Of course, there are also the standard features: the speeches, the ceremonial cake (hey, I was trying to keep to a diet), and the predictable golf jokes. Apparently, every retiree is contractually obligated to spend the rest of their life chasing a tiny white ball in uncomfortable trousers. But the clichés fade quickly. What lingers is the unexpected gratitude, and the warmth of people remembering the things you didn't think mattered.

Now, about the gifts. Corporate gifting is an art form no one has quite mastered. A coffee mug with "Best Boss Ever"? A pen set you may never use because let's be honest, you're already typing this story on a laptop? Maybe I use it when I sign real high value cheques (living in hope, as always)

Rule of thumb: smile, say thank you, and quietly regift, or keep (that's always an option). But I was lucky. I got a few thoughtful ones, gifts that carried meaning, with my family invited to share the moment. Messages poured in from around the world; from colleagues I hadn't spoken to in years. That made it feel global, not just local. Special. Truly special.

And then there was the memory book, absolutely splendid. Pages of photos, notes, doodles, and even a few embarrassing stories (apparently "dark secrets" are fair game when you no longer control the payroll). To top it all, my team staged what they called a "mob dance." I think that's the term. I'm still losing track of the lingo; is it flash mob? Mob squad? Whatever it was, it had more coordination than most project meetings, so I'll call it a success.

And yes, it was emotional. I'm not too proud to admit I teared up. I choked a few times during my speech, fumbling to find words big enough for decades of memories. My kids spoke, which made my heart swell. My wife said a few words, and I'll remember those forever. In that moment, it wasn't just about me stepping out of corporate life, it was about all of us, the family that carried me through it.

When it was done, I felt lighter, fuller, and oddly ready. A chapter closed with laughter, tears, questionable cake, and a surprise dance routine. Not a bad way to bow out.

Timestamp #34: Letting Go of Office Rituals

For years, your life runs on rituals. The morning coffee with colleagues. 9.30 a.m. "quick check-in." The Friday afternoon decompression session, where you try to be on your own in your room. These little anchors give structure to your days, as familiar as your commute or your ID card swipe. And then, almost overnight, they're gone.

I used to walk the floor, hands in my pockets, catching up with people. It wasn't just small talk; it was my personal newsroom. In one lap, I'd get updates on the organisation, the industry, and, of course, a few juicy titbits of gossip. Honestly, I didn't need a newspaper. My team provided a full subscription, covering every section: politics, sports, lifestyle, even the entertainment page.

And every now and then, someone would offer a snack from their desk, usually unhealthy, always irresistible, accompanied by a casual ask for help or advice. Those little exchanges became the rhythm of my day.

At first, I missed them. There's a strange emptiness in those early days of retirement. I'd wander into the kitchen at 11 a.m., half-expecting someone to pop up with a project update I no longer needed to hear. The silence was unsettling.

But slowly, the rituals began to shift. The morning coffee turned into a cup of green tea (with a surprisingly orangey flavour) sipped on the balcony instead of in a meeting room. The Friday ritual morphed into a round of golf or a long walk, where the decompression was about life, not deadlines.

And my old "walk-and-talk" routine? That found a new home too. Now, it's fellow walkers in the park, most of them sporting a fair share of grey hair. Turns out, the world outside offices is full of gossip and stories just as juicy as anything I ever heard in the cafeteria. Stock tips, family drama, holiday planning, it's all there, just with a different set of characters.

That's the thing about rituals. They don't disappear. They evolve. Retirement doesn't leave you adrift; it gives you the freedom to build new rhythms without needing Outlook reminders or meeting invites. The conversations continue, the connections remain. They just happen in different places, with different people, and usually with better (and healthier) snacks.

Timestamp #35: The Last Commute

The commute. Love it or hate it, it becomes part of your identity. For years, it framed your mornings and evenings, sometimes with frustration, sometimes with surprising calm. And then comes the final ride; one last honk-filled memory. You expect to feel liberated. Instead, you find yourself oddly sentimental about traffic lights.

On that last drive, you start noticing details you had ignored for years. The chai stall where steam always curled into the morning air. The billboard that somehow never changed its peeling paint or outdated message. The security guard at the office gate, who never once failed to wave. What was once background noise becomes a victory lap, a slow-motion reminder of the life you lived at full speed.

Even the parking lot feels like a museum of memories. You'd perfected the art of sliding into "your" spot, knowing exactly when to turn, when to reverse, when to stop. Pure muscle memory. You knew which corners of the basement had phone signals, and which were dead zones. You could tell who was in early or burning the midnight oil simply by recognising their cars. In some ways, the parking garage was your attendance sheet.

Then there was the reserved board with your car number. And the parking attendant, who perhaps was also nearing retirement, looked genuinely bewildered when I shook his hand for the last time. He couldn't quite process the idea of me no longer driving in each morning. I slipped him a quiet but generous tip, partly as thanks, partly as acknowledgement that this ritual was ending for both of us.

When it's over, you don't feel only relief. Sure, you're grateful you'll never again be stuck in a traffic jam behind a truck belching fume. But more than that, you feel gratitude for the journeys that shaped you. Gratitude for the chai stalls, the billboards, the handshakes, and even the horns.

Because the commute wasn't just about getting to work. It was part of the story of your working life. And that last ride wasn't an ending. It was a reminder that every mile, even the noisy ones, brought you here.

Timestamp #36: The Last ID Card Scan - That Last Beep

There's something strangely symbolic about that last beep at the office gate. You scan your ID card, the barrier opens as it always has, and it hits you: tomorrow, this little piece of plastic won't matter anymore.

It's just a card. A rectangle of laminate and electronics. But for years, it was your passport to a sense of belonging. That final scan feels less like an entry and more like a curtain call. The show is over. Time to step out of costume.

I often thought about updating the photograph. The one on my card never looked quite like me, and with every passing year, the gap widened. But then again, keeping the younger version had its perks. A scratchy old headshot became a quiet illusion, a way of staying younger every time someone looked me up on the intranet.

And oh, the stories this card carries. The mornings I'd forgotten it at home and had to negotiate with security. The time I got locked out of my bay, arms full of food and coffee, with the card dangling just out of reach. The retractable card holder that snapped at the worst moment. The irritating lanyard that never sat straight. And the darker memory, during the financial crisis, walking in each morning with a small, silent fear: *Would the card still let me through? Would the gates open?*

For something so ordinary, it held extraordinary weight. And once it stops working, no one else cares. The system retires your access, and the card becomes useless, except to you, when nostalgia strikes.

Most people keep theirs as a souvenir, tucked away in a drawer. I did the same. Sometimes, I stumble across it while looking for something else and can't help but laugh. *They really let me run things?*

The last beep isn't just the end of access. It's the quiet signal that a whole chapter has closed. And all that remains is a piece of plastic and the countless stories it unlocks in your memory.

Timestamp #37: Cafeteria Chronicles - The Last Supper

One of the underrated luxuries of office life is the cafeteria. Such a huge variety, I never bothered carrying food from home. Why would I, when every day promised a different adventure? Indian one day, Italian the next, Chinese noodles on Wednesday, Mughlai curries by Friday. If you were feeling fancy, there were "continental" options with vegetables you'd never heard of. And then, of course, the apps arrived, making choice both easier and infinitely harder.

But here's the crazy part: for all the productivity we preached, employees spent an astonishing amount of time just deciding what to eat. For some folks, three meals a day happened in the office, especially with corporate discounting making it cheaper than cooking. In its own way, the cafeteria was the busiest decision-making hub in the building.

It wasn't just about food, though. The dining hall had its own energy, almost like a mood barometer for the organisation. When the markets were down or the quarterly results disappointed, you could feel it in the silence at the tables. Conversations grew hushed, laughter fewer. On good days, the noise rose like a festival bazaar, buzzing, cheerful, unstoppable.

Speaking of festivals, the cafeteria was always the stage. Diwali sweets, Holi colours, Christmas cakes; food became the bridge across teams, hierarchies, and cultures. And of course, there was the unofficial social ritual: swapping lunchbox items. A bit of biryani for a paratha, a spoonful of homemade sabzi traded for a kebab. Food, in India especially, is a unifier. Nothing builds trust faster than someone offering you a piece of their mother's pickle.

Looking back, the cafeteria was more than a place to eat. It was a theatre of stories, friendships, and moods. You went in hungry, came out nourished, sometimes with food, sometimes with gossip, sometimes with unexpected advice from a colleague over sambar.

Retirement takes you out of that hall, yes. But the memory of those meals lingers, not in the taste of the food, but in the flavour of the connections.

Timestamp #38: The Last Green Tea (or Coffee)

Some people needed coffee to function. I needed my little pouches of green magic. By the end, even the pantry staff were part of my crusade. I'd nudge them to experiment with mint, jasmine, lemon, something vaguely called "detox." Before long, we had a mini tea lab bubbling away in the corner of the office, complete with unsolicited reviews and "limited editions."

Like most habits, it started innocently. One cup to wake up. Another mid-morning. A post-lunch reset. And then, somehow, an evening revival before the last meeting. By the time I counted honestly, I was on fifteen cups a day. Colleagues tracked their steps; I tracked teabags.

It wasn't just hydration. It was a ritual. Performance art, even. Standing in the pantry, swirling hot water as if I were auditioning for MasterChef. Adding dramatic pauses while the colour shifted from pale straw to "something vaguely radioactive." That pause gave me cover to chat with a colleague, listen to a rant, or just stare out the window pretending to "reflect strategically."

Then one day, it hit me: this wasn't about tea at all. Doing the math at fifteen cups a day meant hours, maybe months of my career, spent brewing, sipping, waiting. But I don't regret a minute of it.

Those breaks were oxygen. They were tiny reset buttons scattered through the day. They gave me friendships, whispered confessions, and off-the-record advice you'd never hear in a meeting. Deals were discussed, grievances aired, alliances forged, all while dunking a teabag.

Retirement means you'll eventually brew that *last* office cup. And no, you won't remember the flavour as it was never really about the taste. What stays is the pause it offered, the people it gathered, and the reminder that the smallest rituals sometimes take up the largest rooms in memory.

So when I think of career badges of honour, it's not just the promotions or the plaques. It's that humble green pouch, brewing quietly in the background, marking time in ways no performance review ever could.

Timestamp #39: The Email You Reread Before Logging Out

On your last day, you open your inbox one more time. Not to check unread messages that's someone else's problem now but to scroll through the history you've unknowingly archived.

You stumble across an email from years ago. Maybe it's a thank-you note, maybe it's a line of praise after a tough project. You reread it and realise that these were the real rewards. Not the bonuses or the plaques, but the words people sent when you made a difference in their lives.

Scrolling further, you see your first payslip in the system and, for fun, compare it to the most recent one. Progress, certainly. For a brief second, you think of printing them out as souvenirs. Then compliance whispers in your ear, and you wisely steer clear of that thought.

There's also the temptation to count. How many emails did you send over the years? Tens of thousands? Hundreds of thousands? And did you reply to every important one? Probably not, but you tell yourself you did. The goodbye messages, meanwhile, are too many to count. Each one a small reminder that you were part of a community.

Mixed in are the outliers. That one reprimand email, sharp and unforgettable yet a lesson that stayed with you long after the sting faded. Emails from friends who are no longer around, each one suddenly priceless. The monthly credit card statement that reminds you: time to update the billing address. And then the cascade of practical thoughts: which subscriptions, which accounts, which reminders still live here and need to move to a personal email ID.

You linger as long as possible, scrolling, searching, remembering. Because you know this is it, the last time this inbox will belong to you. Eventually, you close it. One last look, one final breath. The laptop shuts with a quiet click.

And no, you don't check "Send/Receive" one final time. Well… maybe just once. Old habits die hard.

Timestamp #40: The Sound of Silence at 10 a.m. the Next Day

The first morning after retirement is strangely unsettling. You still wake up at the usual hour because your body clock doesn't reset overnight. You follow the familiar routine, brush, shower, breakfast, tea. And then… nothing.

At 10 a.m., the realisation lands. There's no meeting invite. No urgent call. No red dot on the inbox screaming for attention. Just silence. For a brief moment, you actually wonder if the Wi-Fi has died.

It feels disorienting. Your body is conditioned to expect noise, to brace for movement, to jump into the rhythm of "what's next." Without it, you feel like a sprinter waiting at the starting line long after the race has been cancelled.

But slowly, almost without noticing, you begin to lean into the quiet. You hear the birds outside, loud in their morning gossip. You notice how the sunlight hits the living room floor in a way you never paused to observe before. You take another sip of tea, not gulping it between calls, but tasting it. And the luxury of *not* refreshing your inbox every five minutes? That's a high no corporate perk can match.

The silence, you realise, isn't absence. It's space. And in that space lies possibility, the chance to decide, rather than react. To choose your own pace instead of running at someone else's.

Of course, let's not romanticise it too much. Sometimes, that 10 a.m. silence is broken not by birdsong but by your spouse handing you a to-do list. Retirement has a way of filling the gaps quickly.

Still, that first 10 a.m. pause marks the beginning of a new rhythm. And if you can sit with the silence long enough, you'll find it's not empty at all. It's the sound of life, waiting for you to step into it.

Phase 5

The Firsts

Early post-retirement experiences. The good, the strange, the confusing

What is Phase 5?

This month is about gentle discovery, not performance.

First Monday without meetings. First lunch on a weekday. First nap without guilt. Expect the pendulum: over-scheduling to prove you're "still productive," then empty days that feel too quiet.

Build a starter kit: three anchors (morning movement, one creative/learning hour, one human connection), one daily "useful" act (for self, family, or community), and one delight (a book chapter, a park bench, brewing coffee properly).

Treat your home like a shared workspace, agree zones and routines that keep love intact. Notice cravings for the old adrenaline; swap them for paced momentum like walks over sprints, deep work over shallow busyness.

Keep experiments tiny and reversible: two trial classes, one volunteer shift, one mentoring coffee. Journal your energy, not achievements.

At the end of Week 4, ask: What felt nourishing? What felt noisy? Keep the first list, shrink the second.

The goal of Phase 5 is to learn your new cadence. When your day feels shaped and not stuffed and you can be alone without feeling abandoned, you're ready for the "nexts."

Timestamp #41: The First Week Without Meetings

It's only been a week, but it feels like my calendar has died and gone to heaven. No recurring check-ins. No "urgent" sync calls. No mysterious invites titled "Quick Chat" that actually meant two hours of PowerPoint slides and someone saying, "Can we circle back on this?" The silence is… suspicious.

The first couple of mornings, I still flinched when I opened my laptop. I half-expected Outlook to leap out with a flood of reminders. My thumb hovered over the phone, waiting for the familiar buzz of Teams or Zoom. Nothing. Instead, the morning stretched out in front of me like an empty road. I didn't quite know what to do with it.

So I experimented. A longer walk. A leisurely breakfast. Even fifteen minutes of just staring at the ceiling and let me tell you, ceilings are far more interesting than I'd ever noticed. Mine has patterns I've ignored for decades. Who knew?

By midweek, the itch faded. I didn't miss the meetings. I missed the people, maybe, and the banter before the agenda, the whispered jokes in the chat, the knowing eye rolls when someone used too much jargon. But politics? The endless debates about synergy, alignment, or "low-hanging fruit"? Never again.

By Friday, a revelation hit me: meetings had become less about progress and more about habit. We filled our days with them because that's what work demanded. Now, without them, my day had space. And in that space, I found something radical: calm.

It's strange that you spend decades complaining about meetings, and then when they vanish, you almost miss the noise. Almost. But not enough to want them back.

So I raised a mug of green tea (my new "team huddle") and marked the score: Retirement 1, Outlook 0. And for the first time in years, Friday felt like a victory without needing a single status update.

Timestamp #42: Your Spouse's First Reaction to You Being Home All Day

No one really prepares you for this. You think retirement is going to be a shared celebration of long breakfasts, unhurried lunches, maybe even a spontaneous midweek movie. And for you, Day One feels like freedom finally delivered.

For your spouse? It feels more like a home invasion.

Suddenly, you're everywhere. In their kitchen. On their sofa. Hovering in the hallway. You've gone from "weekend presence" to "full-time roommate," and they're still adjusting to the new schedule. You, meanwhile, think you're being helpful. You point out how the dishwasher could be loaded more efficiently. You suggest a new system for folding laundry. You even hover around the cooking, offering unsolicited "tips" like a contestant on *MasterChef: Backseat Edition.*

By Day Three, you get *the look.* Married people know it instantly. It's not angry, it's not amused, instead it's the quiet, exhausted glare that says: "I love you, but if you move that saucepan one more time, we're going to have a problem."

By Day Five, the subtle hints become less subtle. "Don't you have golf today?" Or, "Didn't you say you were meeting your friend?" Translation: "Please, for the love of all that's holy, give me back my space."

That's when the penny drops. Retirement isn't just your adjustment. It's theirs too. For years, your spouse ran the house while you ran off to work. They had their rhythm, their space, their quiet hours. Now you're stomping around in the middle of it, and both of you need to learn how to coexist again.

The solution isn't complicated. It's called breathing room. Time apart is as important as time together. Go for that long walk. Take up golf. Read in another room. Space isn't distance, it's oxygen. And love, as it turns out, grows best with oxygen. Especially near the dishwasher.

In the end, retirement doesn't mean being inseparable. It means learning to share life without smothering each other. And when you get that balance right, you discover something better than constant togetherness: companionship that breathes, bends, and still finds joy, even in the kitchen.

Timestamp #43: Overbooking Yourself with "Catch-ups"

The strangest thing about retiring is that your calendar doesn't actually stay empty for long. In fact, it sometimes looks busier than before, only now it's filled with a different kind of meeting. The "catch-up."

It starts innocently. A friend says, "We must grab coffee now that you're free." Another suggests lunch. An old colleague insists on a "quick chat" to hear about this mysterious thing called retirement. Before you know it, your week is a patchwork of breakfasts, brunches, coffees, and dinners. By Thursday, you're wondering if retirement is just a code word for running a food festival.

At first, it's flattering. You feel popular, even indispensable. Everyone wants a piece of your time. But by the third double-shot cappuccino of the day, you begin to realise that this isn't leisure, this is logistics. Your diary may no longer be run by Outlook, but it's still dictating your life, only with more caffeine and fewer spreadsheets.

The conversations themselves are a mixed bag. Some are warm and nostalgic. Some are curious, as people try to decode how you had the courage to step away. And some, let's be honest, are just people fishing for free advice. ("If you were still in the organization, how would you..." Sound familiar?)

The irony, of course, lies in how quickly you fall back into old habits. You set reminders. You check the time. You rush from one café to another, wondering why your feet hurt more than they did during corporate life. Retirement was supposed to mean slowing down, not earning a loyalty card at every coffee chain in the city.

By the end of week two, you've learned an important lesson: overbooking yourself in retirement feels just as exhausting as overbooking yourself at work. The trick is moderation. A couple of meet-ups a week is delightful. More than that, and you start fantasising about an "out-of-office" message again.

So yes, catch-ups are wonderful. They remind you of the networks you built, the friendships you still cherish. But they don't need to happen all at once. Retirement isn't a limited-time offer, it's a marathon, no wait, it's an ultra-marathon. Pace yourself. And maybe switch one coffee for green tea. Your heart will thank you.

Timestamp #44: The Morning You Slept In… Then Felt Aimless

For years, you fantasised about it. No alarm, no snooze button, no mad rush. Just one glorious morning of sleeping in. And finally, retirement delivers. You wake up at 9 a.m., stretch luxuriously, and think: *This is it. This is the dream.*

Then… ten minutes later, the dream wobbles. You shuffle to the kitchen, make yourself tea, and realise you have absolutely nowhere to be. The calendar is blank, the phone is silent, and the day stretches ahead like an empty cricket field with no players.

At first, you try to enjoy it. You linger over breakfast. You flip through the newspaper, even reading the classifieds just to kill time. You check your WhatsApp groups twice, then again, in case someone broke news in the last three minutes. Nothing. Suddenly, sleeping in feels less like freedom and more like standing in quicksand.

This is the paradox of retirement: the very thing you craved, unstructured time, can feel unsettling when it actually arrives. In the office, a free hour was a gift. Outside it, a free day feels like a trap. Without deadlines snapping at your heels, you don't quite know how to move.

I once caught myself asking, *"Should I make another cup of tea? Or is that too ambitious?"* That's when I knew I was in trouble. It wasn't about caffeine. It was about purpose.

That aimlessness isn't failure. It's recalibration. After decades of sprinting, your brain needs time to unlearn the idea that worth equals productivity. Feeling a little lost is simply proof that you're finding a new compass.

So yes, the first few mornings may feel oddly empty. You'll fidget. You'll overthink. You might even polish your shoes for no reason. But eventually, you learn to fill the silence with things you actually choose, maybe a walk, a book, a hobby that doesn't involve Outlook.

Sleeping in is only half the gift of retirement. The other half is waking up, not because you *have* to, but because you *want* to.

Timestamp #45: The Day You Organised Your Bookshelf Instead of a PPT

There was a time when "organisation" meant endless slides, colour-coded charts, and version 4.1 of a deck that no one would ever read again. Hours spent debating fonts and bullet points, only for the big boss to say, "Let's simplify this."

And then retirement happens. Suddenly, you wake up one morning and decide to tackle something else: the bookshelf.

It starts innocently enough. You pull out a dusty novel wedged between annual reports (why did you keep those?). Soon, you're knee-deep in piles of books, magazines, and papers you forgot existed. Unlike a PPT, this doesn't need approvals. No one is asking you to "tighten the executive summary." It's just you, your books, and a surprising sense of satisfaction.

You find management textbooks that once felt like gospel but now read like satire. You stumble upon a half-finished novel you promised you'd get to "when things calm down", almost ten years ago. You even find those "motivational" leadership books gifted at conferences, their bookmarks still stuck at page five.

By the time you're done, the spines are neatly lined, the dust has been wiped clean, and you can actually see the wood of the shelf again. It feels like producing something tangible, something no one will edit or critique. A rare "final version" in a world where you used to live in drafts.

The bookshelf becomes more than furniture. It's a mirror. The novels you loved, the biographies that inspired you, the random travel guides, they tell the story of who you were outside of work. It's a reminder that your life was never just about PowerPoint.

So yes, organising your bookshelf may not sound like an achievement worthy of a LinkedIn update. But in that quiet act, you unlock something better than a quarterly goal: visible progress. And unlike the PPTs, no one will ask you to redo it tomorrow.

Timestamp #46: Still Wearing Work Clothes for No Reason

Old habits die hard. On your first week of retirement, you wake up, shower, and then without thinking, you pull on your neatly pressed trousers and collared shirt. By 10 a.m., you're sitting at home, formally dressed with nowhere to go. The neighbours probably assume you've taken on a secret new role.

It's funny how clothes carry identity. For years, your work wardrobe was your armour. Crisp shirts, polished shoes, even the carefully chosen tie, all signals that you were "ready." Now, the signals point nowhere. There are no meetings to attend, no presentations to impress, no junior colleagues watching your every move. Just you, the sofa, and a very overdressed outfit.

At first, it feels comforting, almost grounding. The routine makes you believe you're still "in the game." But then it starts to feel ridiculous. Why are you ironing shirts to read the newspaper? Why are your shoes polished when the only journey is from the living room to the balcony?

One morning, you catch your reflection in the mirror, a blazer on top, pyjama bottoms below. You laugh, because that's exactly what half your Zoom calls looked like anyway. Retirement, it seems, is just an extension of the hybrid dress code.

Slowly, you ease into change. The ties migrate to the back of the closet. The shoes gather a little dust. Comfort begins to win over formality. A soft T-shirt, loose trousers, and sneakers feel less like "giving up" and more like letting go.

But you never really stop dressing with purpose. The difference is that now the purpose is your own. You dress for a walk, for a golf game, for a dinner with friends, not for a title. Clothes no longer define your authority. They simply follow your life.

And that, strangely, feels like the best promotion yet.

Timestamp #47: Revisiting Old Hobbies (and Discovering New Ones)

One of the myths about retirement is that you'll suddenly have all this time to do the things you love. Dust off the golf clubs, pull out the paintbrushes, lace up the sneakers for gym, easy, right? What nobody tells you is that hobbies don't stay sharp just because you parked them neatly for 20 years.

Take golf. You walk confidently to the first tee, line up your shot, and... splash. The ball dives into the water hazard like it was magnetised. The next one slices into the woods. By the fifth hole, you remember why golf is less about perfection and more about patience.

Painting is no different. You set up the canvas, arrange the colours, and feel like Picasso reborn. Ten minutes later, it looks more like kindergarten art. But the joy isn't in the masterpiece, it's in the mess. With no deadlines and no critics, even crooked brush strokes feel like progress.

Then there's hiking. Your younger self remembers charging up trails with ease. Now, halfway up a modest hill, you're panting, wondering when "scenic route" became code for "cardio punishment." But then you stop, take in the view, and realise that slowing down isn't weakness, it's the whole point.

Swimming offers another humbling lesson. The first few laps feel glorious, the water wrapping you in freedom. By the fifth lap, though, you're gasping and clinging to the edge like a tourist on a banana boat. Still, it's impossible not to smile, there's something liberating about rediscovering the water on your own terms.

Cycling brings its own comedy. You dust off the old bike, tighten the helmet, and set off feeling invincible. Two kilometres in, your legs are burning, and every uphill slope feels like Everest. But coasting downhill, wind in your face, you feel twelve again, creaky knees and all.

Retirement hobbies aren't about mastery. They're about rediscovery. About remembering what it feels like to play, to fail, to laugh at yourself, and to try again anyway. You don't get graded. No one's tracking your performance. The only metric is joy.

So yes, the golf swing is rusty, the paint strokes wobbly, the hiking shoes worn, the cycling muscles unprepared, and the swimming technique questionable. But all of it beats a day of conference calls. Because hobbies remind you of something work often makes you forget: life isn't about results. It's about experience.

Timestamp #48: First Trip as a "Retired" Person

For decades, travel came with admin. Apply for leave, draft a handover note, check that no crisis would explode in your absence, and then the most depressing part: write the dreaded out-of-office message. Even on holiday, you weren't really free. You'd sneak a glance at your inbox, pretend to "just check one thing," and suddenly find yourself on a conference call from a hotel balcony.

Retirement changes all that. The first time you book a trip as a retired person, it feels almost too easy. You pack your bags, zip them shut, and realise there's no draft email to send. No approvals to wait for. No guilty handovers. You just… go.

And when you arrive, the difference is even clearer. Breakfast isn't rushed so you can "make the 9 a.m. call." You linger over pancakes, not slide decks. You explore without thinking about when Wi-Fi will be available. The phone stays in your pocket, not as a leash, but as a camera.

The luggage feels lighter too. Not because you packed less, but because you didn't pack stress. There's no invisible suitcase filled with deadlines and responsibilities tagging along. The freedom is palpable and almost comical.

And then it hits you: *So, this is what vacations were supposed to feel like.* Not "borrowed time" from work. Not a frantic escape to recharge for Monday. But real time, your time, with no expiry date attached.

You sip your tea at an airport café and watch business travellers hunched over laptops, frantically typing. You smile quietly. That used to be you. Now, the only deadline is the boarding gate.

Timestamp #49: Getting Used to "So What Do You Do?"

It's the most common small-talk question in the world: *"So, what do you do?"* For decades, you had a ready-made answer. A title. A company. A neat little line that fit perfectly on a business card and instantly earned nods of approval.

Then retirement arrives, and suddenly, that neat answer vanishes. At your first party, someone asks the dreaded question, and you freeze. You can't exactly say, *"Former Managing Director"* without sounding like you're clinging to a ghost. And saying *"Nothing"* feels both untrue and slightly insulting to yourself.

You're tempted to go for honesty. *"I do naps."* Accurate, yes. LinkedIn-unfriendly, definitely. Or maybe *"I do Tuesdays without alarms,"* which is closer to the truth but still gets you blank stares.

Some retirees cling to the past: *"I was with XYZ for 25 years."* Others inflate hobbies into full-time gigs: *"I'm a golf strategist." "I'm exploring painting as a contemporary discipline."* (Translation: you slice the ball into water hazards and smear acrylics like a toddler.)

We're conditioned to measure ourselves by what we *do*, not who we *are*. Work gave us a label. Without it, the identity feels under construction. But maybe that's the gift of retirement, the chance to answer differently.

Instead of *what* you do, you start answering with *how* you live. You mentor. You walk. You spend time with family. You finally try that cooking class. You learn to waste time gloriously, without apology. The answers don't fit neatly on a nameplate, but they're real.

And sometimes, when you don't feel like explaining, there's always the classic fallback: *"Consultant."* It's vague enough to shut people up, mysterious enough to command respect, and broad enough to cover everything from coaching to binge-watching.

Eventually, you stop worrying about the question. Because retirement teaches you this: your value doesn't need a job title to prove it. And maybe the most satisfying answer of all is the simplest one: *"I do what I want."*

Timestamp #50: Feeling the Absence of Structure

For most of your life, the calendar ran you. Every hour had a slot, every day had a rhythm. Check-ins, town halls, client calls, performance reviews, even "quick coffees" had to be scheduled weeks in advance. The tyranny of Outlook ruled your existence.

And then retirement comes. The calendar clears. The invites vanish. Monday morning looks suspiciously blank. No alarms, no reminders, no "hard stop at 4 p.m." Freedom, in all its glory.

At first, it's intoxicating. You sleep a little longer, linger over breakfast, wander out for a mid-morning walk without guilt. The absence of structure feels like floating, light, untethered, exhilarating.

Then, slowly, the other side creeps in. Floating can feel a lot like drifting. With no anchor points, the days blur together. You find yourself asking, *"Wait, is it Wednesday?"* You open the fridge at 11 a.m., not out of hunger, but out of boredom. You reorganise your desk, then your bookshelf, then wonder if the dog really needs a fourth walk.

The truth is, the structure wasn't just a prison, it was also scaffolding. It gave shape to your time, even when it annoyed you. Without it, you're left staring at hours that stretch like open fields. Beautiful, yes, but also intimidating.

Funnily, I once caught myself considering whether to block "nap time" on my own calendar, just to feel useful. Another day, I almost sent myself a meeting invite titled *"Figure Out Lunch."* Old habits die hard.

But the adjustment isn't about recreating the old grid. It's about designing a rhythm that feels lighter, more deliberate. You don't need back-to-back calls, but you do need anchors, a morning walk, an afternoon swim, an evening chat with friends. Enough scaffolding to stop drifting, without recreating the grind.

And that's when the absence of structure shifts from unsettling to liberating. The calendar doesn't own you anymore. You own the calendar. And if one of your recurring events happens to be "sit on the balcony and watch the world," well, that's still a meeting worth keeping.

Phase 6

Redefining Self

The existential pivot and self-discovery phase

What is Phase 6?

Now we move from novelty to pattern.

The question shifts from "What will I fill time with?" to "What deserves a place in my week?"

Expect a second wobble: the initial high fades and structure matters. Design a simple week: two movement days, two contribution slots (mentoring/volunteering/consulting), two curiosity blocks (class/reading/making), one true blank day.

Protect the blank day; boredom is a doorway, not a defect. Audit commitments: anything that bloats your calendar without feeding your soul gets a gracious "no." Health becomes pragmatic and not a 30-day sprint but a sustainable practice: check-ups, sleep, food that loves you back.

Money conversations mature: shifting from accumulation to allocation towards experiences, learning, and care. Expect identity echoes ("So what do you do?"). Answer with verbs, not nouns: "I write, I teach, I walk."

The goal of Phase 6 is confidence in an unhurried life. When you can design a week that would make "future you" grateful and actually live it, then you're ready to rejoin the world on new terms.

Timestamp #51: Saying "I Used to Be..." Too Often

It slips out before you even notice. Someone asks, "So, what do you do?" and you answer, "Well, I used to be..."

Used to be. Three tiny words that carry the weight of an entire career. For decades, your identity was inseparable from your job title. It was your shortcut introduction at parties, your badge of honour at alumni meets, your easy answers when you didn't feel like explaining yourself. And suddenly, it's in the past tense.

At first, it felt natural, it was almost too comforting. "I used to be a Managing Director." It signals gravitas, credibility, importance. But repeat it often enough, and you start to hear the echo yourself. It sounds less like pride and more like clinging. Like you're introducing a ghost.

And you don't realize fast enough how ridiculous it can get. I once caught myself telling a neighbour, "I used to be in a corporate job." They just nodded politely, probably thinking, *"That explains why he keeps reorganising the housing society committee minutes."* Another time, at a dinner, I rattled off my past roles until my daughter whispered, "Dad, you sound like a LinkedIn profile." Brutal. But accurate.

And yet, there's an emotional truth underneath. Retirement doesn't erase what you *used to be*. It just can't be the headline forever. At some point, you have to shift the story. From past tense to present. From job titles to life choices.

That's the pivot. Learning to say, "I paint." "I play golf." "I mentor." Even, "I nap." Not as filler, but as identity. The trick isn't to deny the past, it's to stop living in it.

So yes, you'll still slip into "I used to be..." every now and then. It's part of the transition, like breaking in a new pair of running shoes. But eventually, you realise the most powerful thing about retirement isn't what you used to be. It's what you get to be now.

Timestamp #52: Sleep as a Luxury

The first shock of retirement isn't silence. It's sleep.

For decades, an alarm clock yanked you into consciousness at ungodly hours. 5:00 a.m. gym, 6:30 a.m. commute, 8:00 a.m. meeting. Even Sundays weren't safe, the body trained itself to twitch awake, already running through ironing clothes, emails, and the next week's battles. It was as if sleep were a suspicious activity that had to be justified: "Yes, I did sleep six hours, but I also checked my inbox at 4 a.m."

And suddenly… nothing. No alarms. No snoozes. No calendar reminders vibrating on the bedside table. Just your body deciding what "enough" means. It's unsettling at first. You open one eye at 4:45am out of habit, expecting the tyranny of Outlook or a flight to catch. Instead, you're greeted by… birds. And the realization that you can roll over and go back to sleep without fear of missing the boss's "quick connect." That freedom is intoxicating.

At first, it feels decadent. Waking up at 7 instead of 5? You want to frame it, announce it on LinkedIn: "Achieved two extra hours of shut-eye: #blessed." Then comes the true indulgence: the afternoon nap. Not the guilty, half-hour power nap at your desk, chin bouncing off your tie while pretending to "read a report." No. This is the unapologetic, drool-on-pillow variety. The kind where you wake up not knowing what day it is but feeling like you've been reborn.

And yet, years of conditioning don't vanish overnight. For weeks, you'll still find yourself wide awake at 4:59 a.m., blinking at the ceiling. But slowly, your body retrains itself. You learn to savour the in-between: lying awake without urgency, drifting off again because you can.

Sleep stops being an obstacle to productivity and becomes the prize itself.

A retiree friend once told me, "I now measure success by how well I sleep." At first, I laughed because surely success had loftier markers than bedtimes. But he was right. Sleep is not laziness; it's healing. It's energy. It's the one resource you spent decades sacrificing for work and are finally reclaiming.

In retirement, productivity isn't about inbox zero or back-to-back meetings. It's eight glorious hours of uninterrupted rest plus one afternoon nap for good measure.

Luxury isn't a Rolex. It's REM.

Timestamp #53: Your First Passion Project Attempt

Every retiree has that list. The passion project you swore you'd start once you had "time." Write a book. Plant a garden. Paint. Launch a podcast. Train for a marathon (ha!). For years, these dreams sat patiently in the background, waiting for their turn.

Then retirement happens, and you finally say: *This is it. Today I begin.*

The first attempt is, frankly, hilarious. If it's gardening, the seeds sprout proudly… before withering like your enthusiasm after week one. If it's writing, you sit at the desk, open a blank page, and spend two hours adjusting the font. If it's painting, you squeeze out colours with grand ambition, only to discover the end result looks like a toddler's revenge on canvas.

The important part isn't that it's clumsy, it's that it's yours. For the first time in decades, you're creating without a boss, a deadline, or a quarterly review. No one is marking your work. No one is saying, *"Can you make version 2.0 by tomorrow?"* You're free to enjoy the mess.

Of course, spouses and friends can't resist commentary. "That's… interesting," they say, staring at your abstract art. "You're so dedicated," they remark, as you pant halfway through a "marathon" training walk. You smile, because you know the point isn't applause, it's rediscovery.

And yes, passion projects often fizzle. The half-finished manuscript, the abandoned blog, the yoga mat gathering dust. But that's okay. Retirement isn't about becoming an overnight expert. It's about giving yourself permission to try. To play. To be a beginner again without shame.

Because here's the truth: even failed passion projects succeed. They remind you that your time is your own now. That you're free to experiment, to stumble, to laugh at yourself. And if one project doesn't stick, there's always another waiting in the wings.

So go ahead and plant the seeds, pick up the brush, lace up the shoes. The first attempt may be clumsy, but it's also the first step into a life where curiosity sets the pace.

Timestamp #54: Who You Spend Time with Now (And Who Fades Out)

Retirement is like turning on a social sieve. Suddenly, you notice who trickles through and who disappears. The office crowd you saw daily? Some vanish the moment your email ID stops working. The WhatsApp groups that once pinged non-stop? They go eerily quiet once you're no longer part of "the fun project."

At first, it stings. You wonder if those friendships were real or just proximity dressed up as camaraderie. Then you realise: it's not betrayal, it's gravity. Work was the orbit that held many of those connections together. Remove the orbit, and only the truly bonded satellites stick around.

The "I'll call you often" promises turn into the occasional festival greeting. Some colleagues only resurface when they need career advice or in one case, a golf buddy for an out of towner. And let's be honest, you don't miss the ones who only ever invited you to meetings, not birthdays.

On the flip side, surprising names pop back in. A college friend you hadn't spoken to in 20 years suddenly feels relevant again. A neighbour becomes a confidant because now you both have time for long evening walks. Even family dynamics shift as you're around more, so you're invited to lunches, a game of bridge, or just sofa conversations you used to miss.

Retirement redraws your social map. The circle shrinks, yes, but it also sharpens. The people who remain are the ones who care about you, not your designation. They don't need your influence or your contacts.

They just enjoy your company even when you're rambling about golf swings or Netflix recommendations.

And that's the unexpected gift. You stop spending time out of obligation and start spending it out of choice. No "political coffees," no "networking lunches." Just genuine conversations that don't require a calendar invite.

So yes, some fade. And that's okay. Because the ones who stay are the ones who matter. Retirement doesn't reduce your circle. It refines it.

Timestamp #55: Accepting That You Don't Have to Be Productive

For decades, productivity was the religion. Every hour accounted for, every task measured, every minute squeezed. "Busy" wasn't just a state, it was a badge of honour. Even weekends came with to-do lists disguised as "family time."

Then retirement shows up, and suddenly, there's no boss, no deadlines, no Monday morning report. And here's the kicker: you still feel guilty when you do nothing. You catch yourself mid-afternoon, sipping tea on the balcony, and think, *"Shouldn't I be... doing something more productive?"* Old habits die harder than corporate jargon.

The first few weeks, you try to trick yourself. You make elaborate to-do lists: organise the bookshelf, re-label the spice jars, plan a three-month garden makeover. By Day Three, you're laughing at yourself because the list looks suspiciously like a disguised version of work.

That's when the realisation hits: retirement isn't about replacing one productivity machine with another. It's about giving yourself permission to simply be. To nap without guilt. To daydream without calling it "strategic thinking." To watch the clouds go by without feeling the urge to log them in Excel.

A retired friend once told me, "I've started calling naps 'horizontal meetings.'" Genius. Another said, "I rate myself on relaxation KPIs, I'm currently exceeding expectations." This is the new metric: joy over output.

Of course, this doesn't mean you stop doing things. You'll cook, garden, read, walk, maybe even paint. But you stop needing everything to add up to an achievement. You stop grading your day by deliverables. The absence of productivity doesn't mean the absence of value, instead it means redefining value.

And here's the truth: not every day has to be a masterpiece. Some days can just… be. You've earned that. After all, you spent decades being "productive." Retirement gives you back the right to be gloriously, unapologetically unproductive. And that, in itself, is progress.

Timestamp #56: Trying Out New Titles - Mentor, Consultant, Volunteer

You think you've left job titles behind, but the world insists on giving you new ones. You're no longer "Managing Director" or "Head of Something Important." Instead, people start introducing you as "mentor," "consultant," or "volunteer." Some even get creative, "retired but dangerous."

At first, it felt strange. Titles were once tied to paychecks, corner offices, and business cards with shiny logos. Now, they're more fluid. One day, you're a mentor, sipping coffee with a young professional who thinks "fax machines" are a myth. Next, you're a consultant, sharing wisdom that sounds suspiciously like common sense. By the weekend, you're a volunteer, distributing food packets and realising you're working harder than you did in corporate life, only this time, you're not paid in stock options, but in smiles.

There's mismatch. I once caught myself saying, "As a consultant..." before realising I hadn't been hired, I'd just given unsolicited advice at a dinner party. Another time, I signed up for a volunteer gig and spent the afternoon moving chairs. Apparently, my transferable skill set now includes furniture relocation.

But here's the emotional core: these titles aren't about status. They're about service. They're not designed to impress others. They're meant to remind you and sometimes reassure you that you still have a role, a place, a way to contribute.

The beauty is, you get to choose which hats to wear and when. Want to mentor? Great. Want to disappear into the hills with a hiking stick?

Also great. There's no HR system forcing you to "update your goals" anymore.

Eventually, you realise the best title is no title at all. You don't need a label to validate your day. But if the world insists on one, go ahead and invent your own. My personal favourite? "Professional Human Being." Business cards pending.

Timestamp #57: Joining a Class Full of Younger People

Nothing humbles you faster than walking into a classroom after retirement. You're excited about a new skill, new community, maybe even a long-postponed passion. Then you look around and realise: everyone else is young enough to be your intern. Or worse, your child.

At first, you try to blend in. You sit quietly, hoping no one notices the grey hair. But then the instructor says, "Pair up with someone your age," and the room goes awkwardly silent. One kind student offers you a chair like you're their visiting uncle. Congratulations! you've just become the class elder.

They finish assignments in minutes while you're still figuring out the app's login. Their idea of research is Google Scholar. Yours is cross-referencing three books and printing notes in 14-point font. When you raise your hand and answer a question, the instructor says, "Great perspective!" which is code for, *"Thank you for reminding us dinosaurs still roam the earth."*

But here's the flip side: it's exhilarating. You're surrounded by energy, ideas, slang you barely understand, and a pace that forces you out of your comfort zone. You realise you're not here to compete but you're here to learn differently. And sometimes, to laugh at yourself when you confuse memes with modules.

One day, a fellow student leans over and says, "You've got so much experience and we learn a lot from your stories." That's when it clicks. You may be slower on the tools, but you bring something valuable: perspective. Not the kind found in textbooks, but the kind earned in boardrooms, airports, and yes, failed projects.

So, you stop trying to keep up and start contributing differently. You share, you listen, and you absorb. And slowly, the age gap becomes irrelevant. You're not "the old guy in class." You're just another learner, showing that curiosity has no expiry date.

Besides, let's be honest: nothing makes you feel younger than being around people who still think turning 30 is "the end."

Timestamp #58: Noticing Your Health Differently

During your working years, health was something you outsourced to annual check-ups and the corporate gym membership you rarely used. Retirement changes that. Suddenly, you're not just noticing deadlines, you're noticing blood pressure numbers. You're not tracking KPIs anymore; you're tracking steps on a fitness app.

It sneaks up on you. You bend to pick something up and hear a sound. It's not the floor creaking, it's your knees. You wake up without an alarm, yet your back still stages a protest. The most shocking discovery? Reading glasses multiply in your home like rabbits, yet you can't find one when you actually need it.

But health awareness isn't all grim. In fact, it becomes oddly motivating. You finally have time to walk daily, swim laps, or cycle without pretending it's "networking exercise." You experiment with yoga and laugh at yourself when you can't tell a downward dog from a collapsing tent. Even food takes on new meaning. Suddenly, turmeric feels less like a spice and more like a miracle drug.

Friends compare cholesterol scores the way they once compared bonuses. Someone boasts about running 10k; you're just proud you survived 10 minutes on the treadmill without pulling something. A retired buddy tells you, "Our bodies are now high-maintenance subscriptions. Forget to renew, and you're in trouble."

Yet beneath the jokes lies a quiet truth: health becomes the real wealth of retirement. You don't have to train for marathons or drink kale smoothies by the gallon. You just have to care and do that consistently. Because all the time and freedom in the world mean little if you can't enjoy them.

So yes, you'll notice aches that weren't there before. You'll attend more doctor visits than board meetings. But you'll also celebrate small victories like a long walk without breathlessness, a morning without stiffness, a meal that actually makes you feel good.

And maybe, just maybe, you'll learn to treat your body with the same respect you once gave your job. Because unlike careers, this is one subscription you can't afford to cancel.

Timestamp #59: Questioning Your Previous Pace

How on earth did I live at that speed for so long?

Back then, your days were a blur of alarms, commutes, meetings stacked like dominoes, late-night emails, rinse, repeat. You thought it was normal to eat lunch at your desk while answering calls and drafting a presentation. You thought being "back-to-back" was a badge of honour, not a diagnosis.

Then one day, you wake up retired and realise you've been running a marathon at sprint pace for decades. Now, when you stroll through the park at 10 a.m., watching others rush to work, you think, *why was I competing in the corporate Olympics when all I needed was a good walk and a sandwich?*

You once measured your value by how many meetings you survived in a day. Now, your big achievement is organising the bookshelf without breaking a sweat. You used to say, "I'll sleep when I'm dead." Now you say, "I'll nap because I'm alive." Perspective.

But it's not just about slowing down, it's about rethinking what pace even means. Faster didn't always mean better. That project you rushed to finish at midnight? No one remembers. The relationships you didn't rush through? Those are what remain.

Of course, the adjustment takes time. For weeks, you may feel guilty if your calendar isn't packed. A free afternoon looks suspicious, like you forgot something. Slowly, though, you begin to embrace it. You realise not every day has to be "maximised." Sometimes the best use of time is no use at all.

The emotional punch is this: questioning your old pace isn't about regret. It's about gratitude. You survived it. You did well. And now you get to choose a different rhythm, one that doesn't leave you gasping for air.

So when people ask, "Don't you miss the hustle?" you can laugh and say, "Not at all. These days, I walk at a pace where I can actually notice the flowers. Turns out, they've been there all along."

Timestamp #60: Getting Comfortable with Being Uncomfortable

No one tells you that retirement is basically a masterclass in discomfort. Not physical discomfort though, yes, your knees may file the occasional complaint but the emotional kind. The discomfort of empty calendars. The awkward silence when someone asks, "So, what do you do?" The unsettling realisation that you no longer have a neatly packaged identity to flash like a business card.

At first, you try to fight it. You fill your days with lunches, projects, and overzealous "catch-ups." You Google hobbies like you're applying for them. You even toy with the idea of starting a blog called *"Retired but Relevant."* (Don't. Just don't.) Anything to avoid that weird, itchy space of not knowing what comes next.

But here's the twist: discomfort is where the magic starts. It's the gap between who you were and who you're becoming. And yes, it feels awkward. Like showing up at a party where you don't know anyone, only to realise the host is… you.

The humour is in how ridiculous it gets. I once blocked three afternoons in my calendar under the noble title *"strategic exploration."* Translation: I stared at the ceiling, wondering if I should learn a new language, Spanish maybe, or just rewatch old cricket matches. Another day, I found myself reorganising the cutlery drawer and thought, *"This is my legacy now."*

But slowly, you stop panicking. You lean into the not-knowing. You discover that being uncomfortable isn't fatal instead, it's freeing.

Because once you accept that you don't need all the answers, you give yourself permission to experiment. To try, fail, laugh, and try again.

The truth is: you've done discomfort before. Remember your first job? First leadership role? First time speaking in public? You figured it out then, and you'll figure it out now. Retirement is just another first.

So yes, it's uncomfortable. But maybe that's the point. Growth never happens in the cushy seats. It happens when you squirm a little, wobble a little, and eventually realise you're standing taller than before.

Phase 7

Conversations & Community

The social ecosystem of retirement shifts and redefines itself

What is Phase 7?

Retirement edits your social graph.

Some ties fade; others deepen; new ones surprise you at the park, club, class, or café. This phase asks you to move from default convenience (colleagues) to deliberate belonging (companions).

Curate three circles: Nourishers (old friends who know your story), Explorers (new people linked by interests), and Bridgers (younger folks' you mentor or learn from).

Replace "We must catch up" with one concrete plan a week.

At home, renegotiate presence: being around isn't the same as being available. Agree signals for focus vs. connection, and celebrate small rituals like weekday breakfasts, evening walks, headphone hours.

Practice generous attention: ask better questions, listen longer, share stories not sermons. If you feel invisible in rooms that used to orbit you, enjoy the superpower: observation without obligation.

The goal of Phase 7 is intentional companionship. When your calendar shows fewer names but richer conversations and your household feels more like a team than a traffic jam, then you're ready to turn inward again and ask, "What gives this season meaning?"

Timestamp #61: Who Still Calls You (And Who Doesn't)

Retirement has a funny way of shrinking your call log. Back in the day, your phone buzzed like a beehive between bosses, team members, vendors, clients, even the IT guy reminding you to reset your password. Every ping felt urgent. Every missed call felt like a potential crisis.

Then you retire. And suddenly, silence. The phone that once lived at 2% battery now goes three days without a charge. At first, you panic, did the network die? Did you accidentally block the world? Then it dawns on you: no, you're just not in the loop anymore.

People you thought you couldn't go a day without hearing from vanish like smoke. The colleague who called you thrice a day now doesn't even send a WhatsApp forward. Meanwhile, your mom still calls daily to ask if you've eaten. Some constants never change.

But there are pleasant surprises too. A few people, the ones who really mattered still call. Not to discuss deliverables, but to check in. To share a laugh. To ask about golf, or movies, or just life. Those calls feel richer, warmer, less transactional. They're not about "What can you do for me?" but "How are you doing?"

Of course, spam calls thrive. Retirement doesn't exempt you from the "Congratulations, you've won a credit card" brigade. The difference? Now you have time to mess with them. When they ask, "Sir, do you work?" you can reply, "No, I've graduated." Confuses them every time.

The emotional truth is this: retirement redraws your contact list. Many numbers fade into irrelevance. A few become lifelines. And in the silence between the rings, you learn something important: you were never defined by the quantity of calls, but by the quality of connections.

So the next time your phone doesn't buzz, don't take it as an absence. Take it as space. Space you can now fill with people who call not because they have to, but because they want to.

Timestamp #62: Talking to Younger Professionals as a Peer, not a Boss

Here's an odd shift retirement brings: you're suddenly in conversations with younger professionals where you're no longer the boss. No reporting lines. No "let's circle back." Just two people talking, side by side.

At first, it felt strange. Decades of habit make you want to default to *manager mode*. You nod sagely, prepare to summarise action points, maybe even assign follow-ups. Then you catch yourself. Wait, you don't have a team anymore. You're not here to delegate. You're here to *listen*.

A young professional once told me, "I love your vintage perspective." Vintage! Not experienced, not wise, vintage. Like I'm a bottle of wine. Another time, I slipped into old habits and said, "I'll look at it and approve this later." Approve what? Their career choices? Retirement humbles you in the funniest ways.

But once you let go of the "boss hat," the conversations get richer. They're not guarded around you because you're not their evaluator anymore. You hear fresh ideas, unfiltered worries, ambitions that haven't yet been worn down by quarterly targets. You become more of a sounding board than a scorekeeper.

You learn as much as you share. They tell you about tools and trends you've never heard of. You tell them about mistakes and recoveries they haven't lived through yet. It's an exchange, not a hierarchy.

You realise your worth doesn't come from authority, instead it comes from connection. And when you speak as a peer, not a boss, your words often land deeper because they're free from agenda.

So yes, sometimes you'll miss the power of being "the decision-maker." But you'll also discover the joy of being "the fellow traveller." Retirement gives you the gift of shedding the armour of hierarchy and stepping into conversations as your unfiltered self.

Besides, when a 25-year-old asks you for advice and then calls you "chill," you know you've done something right.

Timestamp #63: Mentoring Without Fixing

The biggest adjustment when you retire and slip into the mentor role? Realising you're not the fixer anymore. For decades, that was your identity. To spot a problem, solve it, move on to the next. You were paid (well) to make things happen.

Then one day, someone younger comes to you for advice. They pour their heart out about a tricky boss, a career decision, or whether to take a job with free lunch but fewer benefits. Your instincts kick in. You want to say, *"Here's what you should do. Step one, step two, done."* The fixer in you is alive and kicking.

But retirement teaches you something new: mentoring isn't about handing out ready-made answers. It's about asking questions, nudging, sharing stories, and letting them figure out their own path. In other words, you guide without grabbing the steering wheel.

Interestingly, I once caught myself sketching a full-blown action plan on a napkin during coffee with a young professional. They looked at me politely, then said, "Thanks… but I just wanted to vent." Ouch. Lesson learnt: sometimes the best advice is simply listening and nodding.

And honestly, it's freeing. When you stop trying to fix, the pressure lifts. You don't have to prove your brilliance anymore. You don't have to carry the weight of outcomes. You just share what you know, and let them adapt it …. or ignore it. Either way, your job is done.

The emotional upside is big too. You start seeing mentoring less as "transferring wisdom" and more as "holding space." You're not responsible for their decisions. You're just part of their thinking process. And often, that's enough.

So yes, your fixer days are behind you. But your mentoring days? They're just beginning. And if you can laugh at yourself when you slip into "boss mode" accidentally, you'll find that mentoring without fixing is actually easier and, dare I say, more rewarding.

Besides, when they succeed later and say, "You helped me think differently," that feels far better than, "You gave me a to-do list."

Timestamp #64: When You Meet Someone on a Similar Path

Retirement can feel a bit like wandering into uncharted territory. You've packed your bags, left the office behind, and now you're figuring out this new world of time, choices, and endless mornings. Then, one day, you bump into someone else who's also retired and suddenly, you're not alone in the wilderness.

The conversation starts cautiously. "So, how's retirement treating you?" It's the retired person's equivalent of *"How's the weather?"* But within minutes, you're comparing notes like old colleagues at a reunion. The first Monday without meetings. The struggle of explaining "what you do" now. The awkward moments with spouses who aren't thrilled to have you home *all the time.*

You joke about your alarm clock collecting dust, about how grocery shopping on a Tuesday afternoon feels oddly rebellious, about how your new "team meetings" consist of the neighbours on their morning walks. There's laughter in recognising the absurdities only another retiree understands.

But beneath the humour, there's comfort. This person gets it. They understand the weird cocktail of freedom and uncertainty. They've wrestled with the same questions: Am I doing enough? Am I doing too much? Should I really be this excited about a well-organised bookshelf?

Sometimes these encounters blossom into new friendships; golf partners, walking buddies, even travel companions. Sometimes it's just a passing chat that leaves you lighter, reassured that you're not the only one Googling "how to fill your days after 60." Either way, it's a connection.

And that's the quiet gift of meeting someone on a similar path: it reminds you that retirement isn't just an individual journey. It's a shared human experience. You may walk it differently, one person chasing grandkids, another chasing marathons but the road is familiar.

So when you do meet a fellow traveller, don't just nod and move on. Swap stories, swap tips, swap laughs. Because nothing makes the new terrain feel less daunting than knowing someone else is mapping it too and occasionally, also getting lost.

Timestamp #65: Attending Alumni Events with a Different Lens

Alumni events used to be networking goldmines. You went armed with business cards, polished small talk, and a mental pitch about your latest role. The game was simple: who's moved up, who's switched companies, who's hiring?

Retirement flips that lens. Suddenly, you're not scanning name tags for opportunities. You're scanning faces for memories. That guy? You once copied his assignments. That woman? She always organised the best festival parties. You're no longer chasing LinkedIn connections, instead you're chasing nostalgia.

At a recent alumni meet, someone asked me, "So, what are you doing now?" I proudly said, "I'm retired." Their response: "Oh... good for you," followed by the polite silence reserved for people who've exited the rat race. Five minutes later, another batchmate whispered, "How did you pull it off?" Retirement envy is real; it just wears polite disguises.

The real shift is how you engage. You're no longer measuring yourself against corporate ladders. You're not worried about sounding impressive. You're free to ask real questions: How's your family? What are you enjoying outside of work? What have you rediscovered about yourself? Alumni events become less about resumes and more about reunions.

You meet someone who looks far older than you and think, *"Retirement suits me better."* Or someone who looks far younger and you think, *"What's their skincare routine?"* The hierarchy of titles is gone, but the hierarchy of waistlines and hairlines? That remains fully in play.

The emotional payoff is this: alumni events remind you of the journey. Not just the job titles, but the people, the friendships, the silly stories that shaped you. Retirement gives you the luxury of enjoying these moments without rushing back to catch a late-night flight or an early meeting.

So next time, walk in without business cards. You don't need them anymore. What you carry now is lighter, more lasting: stories, laughter, and maybe a selfie with the friends who still care.

Timestamp #66: Conversations With Your Spouse Now That You're Around More

No retirement brochure tells you: when you stop working, your spouse doesn't automatically start celebrating. Suddenly, you're in their space.

All. The. Time.

Conversations shift. At first, you're enthusiastic. "Let's have breakfast together every day!" you declare. By Day 3, you're being gently reminded that not every meal needs a running commentary. One morning, I offered unsolicited thoughts on how the toast could be crisper. That was the day I learned the true meaning of *the look.*

You ask, "What's the plan for today?" as though retirement comes with an itinerary. Your spouse replies, "Same as yesterday, except without you hovering." You suggest rearranging furniture or reorganising the pantry, and suddenly they're Googling part-time jobs for *you.*

But beneath the jokes lies something real. Retirement doesn't just change your rhythm, it changes theirs. They've built their own routines, their own quiet spaces, while you were busy in meetings. Now you're back, expecting to slide in seamlessly. Spoiler: it takes negotiation.

The conversations evolve. You talk more about travel dreams, family plans, even small things like trying a new recipe or walking in the evenings. There are laughs, debates, compromises, sometimes over big things, sometimes over trivial ones like TV remote control rights. And slowly, you rediscover each other not just as "co-managers of the household," but as companions with shared time again.

Of course, space remains essential. Golf, walks, books, hobbies, anything that ensures you don't trip over each other's sanity. A retired friend gave me the best advice: "The secret to a happy marriage post-retirement? Two sets of headphones."

The emotional payoff is this: conversations with your spouse deepen. They're no longer squeezed between conference calls or cut short by late-night emails. They stretch, wander, and sometimes end with laughter over nothing at all.

And that's the hidden gift of retirement, not more words, but better ones.

Timestamp #67: Micro-Adventures

Big adventures are Instagram-friendly. But retirement teaches you that the little ones are often better.

You don't need to scale Everest or book a round-the-world cruise to feel alive. Sometimes it's enough to take the city bus all the way to the end of the line just to see where it goes. Or finally step inside that museum you've walked past for twenty years. Or order the dish you can't pronounce at the hole-in-the-wall café where the chairs wobble and the chutney is unforgettable.

These micro-adventures don't demand luggage, boarding passes, or spreadsheets disguised as itineraries. They demand only one thing: curiosity. And curiosity, it turns out, is the cheapest ticket to joy.

At first, you feel ridiculous. You were once a jet-setting executive, clocking air miles, lounge points, and hotel loyalty tiers like medals of honour. Now you're giggling because you discovered a second-hand bookshop tucked behind the post office. But that's exactly the point. Retirement lets you unlearn the idea that adventure must be expensive, exotic, or exhausting.

A retired friend of mine calls it "weekday wonder." You can wander into a botanical garden on a Tuesday morning while everyone else is stuck in a Zoom call. You can sit on a park bench and count pigeons as if they were your personal Netflix series, slow-moving, low-budget, and strangely addictive.

Sometimes the micro-adventure is as simple as walking down a street you never had "time" for, or catching up with a stranger over shared chai at a roadside stall. These moments don't fill a scrapbook, but they fill you with something rarer, lightness.

Micro-adventures don't need planning or performance. There's no need to "leverage vacation days" or update your out-of-office reply. You just step outside and let the world surprise you.

The payoff is subtle but powerful. You go to bed smiling. Not because you ticked off another KPI or hit a quarterly target, but because you remembered the world is bigger, funnier, and friendlier than the narrow corridor of your old calendar.

Micro-adventures are the new milestones. Who knew a bus ride, a plate of momos, or a quiet Tuesday in the park could feel like freedom?

Timestamp #68: Family Time: Too Much, Too Little, Just Right

One of the myths of retirement is that it automatically means "more family time." The picture looks perfect: long lunches, warm conversations, kids dropping by often, grandkids (if you started really early. We did not.) climbing all over you, and everyone thrilled you're around. Reality, as always, has different plans

At first, you dive in enthusiastically. Breakfast with your spouse, check. Afternoon call with the kids, check. Surprise visits to relatives, double check. But after a while, you notice the cracks. Your kids are busy as they have their own careers, their own meetings, their own "quick syncs." You can't just waltz into their schedules like you're booking a conference room.

Then your "quality time" becomes a bit too much. I once offered to help my son with some college assignments. Within 10 minutes, he gently suggested, "Dad, why don't you… supervise from the sofa?" Translation: you're in the way. My spouse has said the same thing about cooking. Apparently, my "input" on spice levels is not welcome.

Then there are moments when it feels too little. Weeks pass without the kids visiting. Calls are shorter than you'd like. You realise family time isn't a constant stream, it's a rhythm. Sometimes you're in sync, sometimes you're on your own.

But the balance does come. You learn that "just right" family time isn't about frequency. It's about quality. A Sunday dinner filled with laughter. A midweek walk with your spouse. A holiday where you actually enjoy each other instead of checking emails.

The emotional truth? Retirement shifts family dynamics. You're not the provider anymore, at least not in the same way. You're not the absentee who's "always busy." You're present. Sometimes too present. Sometimes not enough. But you're there and that presence, even in small doses, is what counts.

So the trick is simple: don't smother, don't vanish. Find the middle ground where family time feels like a gift, not a burden. Because one day, you'll look back and realise these were the moments that mattered most. Even the ones where you were politely told to "stay out of the kitchen."

Timestamp #69: Hosting Your First Weekday Lunch

There's something deliciously rebellious about hosting a weekday lunch after retirement. For decades, weekdays meant rushing through meals, balancing sandwiches with spreadsheets, or eating in a cafeteria that smelled vaguely of tandoori chicken. Then one Tuesday, you find yourself setting the table at noon, inviting friends over with no Outlook calendar, no "working lunch" agenda, just food and company.

At first, it feels surreal. You're halfway through laying out cutlery when you realise: this would have been your "strategy call" slot. Now, the only strategy is whether to serve dal before or after the paneer. By the time guests arrive, you're already giddy with the freedom of it all.

Everyone shows up looking slightly guilty, like kids bunking school. They whisper, "This feels so strange... eating lunch on a Tuesday!" as if the Productivity Police will come knocking. Someone even joked, "Shouldn't we be sending out minutes of this meeting?"

And then comes the food. Unlike work lunches, where you nibble politely while watching the clock, weekday retirement lunches stretch luxuriously. There's no rush to get back to calls. Dessert isn't an afterthought, it's mandatory. Someone orders a second chai just because they can. You sit back, thinking: this is what eating was meant to feel like.

Of course, there are mishaps. I once overestimated my cooking skills and nearly poisoned everyone with an "experimental curry." Lesson learnt: ordering in is also a form of hosting. Another time, the conversation went so long that guests forgot they had post lunch errands to do, resulting in a frantic scramble of car keys and half-packed leftovers.

But weekday lunches aren't really about food. They're about connection. They remind you that life doesn't have to be confined to weekends. That you can create joy in the middle of an ordinary day. And that retirement's real luxury isn't free time but it's the freedom to spend it how you like.

So go ahead, host that lunch. Laugh, eat, linger. Because sometimes, the best meetings are the ones without an agenda and with dessert.

Timestamp #70: When Someone Asks You for Career Advice

Retirement doesn't erase your reputation. People still remember you as the "boss," the "mentor," or the person who somehow survived twenty budget cycles without losing their mind. Which is why, sooner or later, someone usually younger, bright-eyed, and slightly anxious will look you in the eye and ask, "Can I get your advice on my career?"

At first, it felt flattering. You sit up straighter, ready to channel decades of wisdom. But the corporate playbook you once lived by doesn't always fit their world anymore. They talk about job-hopping, remote-first companies, or side hustles that sound like hobbies with a logo. You're tempted to say, *"Back in my day..."* but stop yourself. You don't want to sound like a human history lesson.

So you improvise. You share stories instead of strategies. You tell them about the time you took a risk and it paid off and then the time it didn't. You admit to mistakes. You laugh at the absurdities, like how you once thought fax machines were the pinnacle of efficiency. They laugh too, partly because they've never seen a fax machine.

The generational gap is real. They ask, "Should I take this start-up role?" and you think, *"Do their parents know about this?"* They say, "I don't want to be tied down to one job forever," and you recall spending 20 years at the same company. Worlds apart, yet the core questions about growth, purpose, balance are exactly the same.

The emotional truth? Career advice in retirement isn't about giving answers. It's about offering perspective. It's about reminding them that careers aren't linear, mistakes aren't fatal, and success doesn't always look like the next title. Sometimes the best thing you can say is, "It'll work out, maybe not how you planned, but how it's meant to."

And here's the kicker: while they think you're helping them, they're helping you too. These conversations keep you connected, curious, and just a little relevant.

So the next time someone asks for career advice, don't dust off the old rulebook. Share a story, crack a joke, and remind them: even retirees are still figuring things out.

Phase 8

Mindset and Meaning

Internal transformation begins

What is Phase 8?

With social dust settling, the deeper questions arrive: What is usefulness without a hustle? Who am I without applause?

Meaning here is less a grand mission, more a steady orientation: doing things that are good *for* you and good *beyond* you.

Define three forms of contribution: Hands (practical help), Head (experience/teaching), Heart (presence/care). Choose one small, repeatable act in each bucket. Reframe ambition from scale to depth: fewer people, greater impact.

Let health be identity-supporting, not weight-obsessing. Expect ghosts of old KPIs, status longings. Greet them; don't feed them.

Curate your inputs: less doomscrolling, more deep reading; fewer hot takes, more long walks.

Build a simple reflection habit: weekly notes on what felt meaningful and what felt performative.

The goal of Phase 8 is coherence: your days align with your values more often than not.

When you can answer "How are you?" with something truer than "busy" and feel calm saying it, you're ready to take stock of the whole year.

Timestamp #71: The Joy of Unstructured Thinking

In corporate life, thinking was never really free. It came with frameworks, slides, and deadlines. "Think outside the box" usually meant *inside a different box, due by Friday at 5 p.m.* Even your so-called "brainstorms" were scheduled, colour-coded, and served with soggy sandwiches.

Retirement changes all that. Suddenly, you're free to think without an agenda. No bullet points, no KPIs, no boss popping in to ask, "Where's the deck?" You find yourself staring out of a window, watching the way sunlight shifts across the floor, and realising that this counts as thinking now.

At first, it felt weird. You catch yourself reaching for a notebook to capture "action points" from your daydreams. Old habits die hard. One afternoon, I even tried to categorise my random thoughts into "short term" and "long term." That's when I knew I needed help or at least more tea.

It gets messy. You start out pondering life's big questions: What gives life meaning? Should I write that book? .... and five minutes later you're wondering why all missing socks do not vanish in pairs. Your mind meanders like a lazy river, and for the first time in decades, that's not only okay, it's welcome.

There is a secret gift in there: unstructured thinking isn't useless. It's liberating. Without the constant pressure to be "productive," your ideas stretch in directions they never could before. A silly doodle sparks a memory. A random musing turns into a plan. Even boredom becomes fertile ground for creativity.

You rediscover that your mind isn't just a tool for work, it's a playground. You don't need a PowerPoint to validate your thoughts. You don't need sign-offs to chase a curiosity. You can simply let your brain wander and see where it goes.

So yes, your thinking may look suspiciously like staring into space. But don't underestimate it. Retirement gives you back the freedom to think for the sheer joy of it. And sometimes, the best ideas arrive not in a boardroom, but in a hammock.

Timestamp #72: Letting Go of "I'm Not Useful Anymore"

One of the sneakiest doubts that creeps in after retirement is this: *Am I still useful?*

For decades, your value was obvious. You had a title, a team, and an inbox full of people who couldn't move without your approval. You signed things. You fixed things. You were needed. Then one day, you're not. Your phone stops buzzing, your desk is cleared, and your corporate "usefulness" evaporates overnight.

At first, it feels like being uninvited from a party you helped organise. You scroll through LinkedIn, watching ex-colleagues announce promotions, and wonder, *What's my role now?*

My son once asked me to help him set up a printer. After 20 minutes of failure, he said, "Wow, Dad, didn't you run a whole department?" Point taken. Another time, an elderly neighbour asked for "your time," but what they really needed was someone tall enough to change a lightbulb. So yes, you're still useful, just in very different ways.

There is a shift. Emotional. Usefulness doesn't disappear. It just changes form. You're not the boss anymore, but you might be the mentor. You're not closing deals, but you're opening doors for others. You're not drafting strategy, but you're sharing stories that spark perspective. Sometimes your usefulness is as simple as being present for your family, your community, or yourself.

The hardest part is letting go of the old definition. For years, usefulness was tied to output, results, and recognition. Retirement asks you to embrace a softer version: being valued not for what you produce, but for who you are.

And slowly, you learn to laugh at the thought that you're "not useful anymore." Because usefulness isn't a corporate deliverable but it's the way you make people feel, the help you offer, the encouragement you give.

So yes, your days of approving budgets are gone. But if you can make someone smile, share a piece of hard-earned wisdom, or finally master the Wi-Fi router, trust me, you're still very, very useful.

Timestamp #73: Learning to Be Still

Stillness is a skill no one teaches you in corporate life. In fact, stillness was practically outlawed. If you were sitting quietly at your desk, someone would inevitably ask, *"Busy?"* and you'd immediately click furiously at your keyboard just to prove you were.

Then retirement arrives. Suddenly, there's no one measuring your output, no boss lurking with a "quick question," no endless stream of emails demanding attention. You sit in your chair with a cup of tea... and that's it. Just you, the tea, and silence.

At first, it's unnerving. You feel guilty, like you've been caught bunking class. The voice in your head whispers, *"Shouldn't you be doing something?"* The old reflex kicks in and you reach for your phone, check the news, fiddle with the TV remote. Anything to fill the quiet.

I once sat down intending to "practice being still." Five minutes later, I was reorganising the sock drawer. Another time, I tried meditation. The app said, "Focus on your breath." Ten seconds in, I was thinking about whether I had enough milk for tomorrow's chai.

Learning to be still isn't about switching off your thoughts. It's about noticing them without running away. It's giving yourself permission to do nothing and realising that "nothing" can actually be nourishing. The mind, like the body, needs rest. And for the first time in decades, you can finally give it that.

Slowly, the stillness becomes less scary. You start enjoying the sound of birds outside, the feel of morning light, the rhythm of your own breathing. You discover that being still doesn't mean being stagnant, it means being present.

And once you get the hang of it, stillness becomes a kind of superpower. It calms the noise, sharpens perspective, and reminds you that life isn't always about motion. Sometimes, it's about sitting quietly and realising that this moment; tea in hand, no alarms, no emails is exactly enough.

Timestamp #74: Rediscovering Local Spaces

Work made you a tourist in your own city. You zipped between home, office, airport, and conference rooms with surgical precision. The neighbourhood was just background scenery, a blur outside the car window. Suddenly, the world at your doorstep starts waving back.

One morning you pause at the tea stall you've ignored for years. The vendor squints, recognises you, and asks, "Long leave, sir?" You laugh, order a chai, and realise you've just become a regular. The corner grocery store owner tells you stories about his father's shop you never knew. Even the street dog who once ignored you now escorts you faithfully to the park and back.

The rediscovery is part comedy, part revelation. You once bragged about flying to London for a three-day meeting. Now you're giddy because you found a new samosa shop three lanes away. It's humbling, almost embarrassing and deeply satisfying.

Local spaces transform when you're not sprinting past them. The park isn't just grass; it's a stage for gossip groups, yoga cliques, and badminton duels. The community library isn't dusty irrelevance; it's an unexpected portal of calm. You find yourself listening longer, noticing more.

The truth is, retirement doesn't shrink your world. It expands it sideways, into overlooked corners and ordinary wonders. Travel brochures can wait. Sometimes the best adventure is hidden behind the milk booth around the corner.

Timestamp #75: Redefining Success

For most of your career, success came with clear markers. Promotions, titles, bonuses, plaques, maybe even a slightly larger cubicle. You knew when you'd "made it" someone handed you a new business card or invited you to meetings you didn't understand.

Retirement scrambles that scoreboard. There are no appraisals, no salary hikes, no trophies for "Best Use of PowerPoint Transitions." The first time someone asks, "So what's keeping you busy these days?" you realise your old answers don't fit. Success can't be measured in quarterly reports anymore.

At first, this feels unsettling. You're wired to chase benchmarks, so you invent new ones: how many steps you walked, how many books you finished, how many cupboards you organised. One friend even bragged about hitting a "personal best" of three naps in a single day. Hey, milestones are milestones.

How absurd can these new measures really get? I once proudly told my spouse I'd "cleared my inbox." She raised an eyebrow and said, "That's because you don't get emails anymore." Fair point. Another time, I caught myself timing how quickly I could solve a Sudoku. Clearly, old habits die hard.

But then something shifts. You begin to see success differently. It's not about output anymore, it's about outcome. Did you laugh today? Did you spend time with someone you care about? Did you feel healthy, engaged, curious? Success becomes less about "climbing" and more about "living."

The emotional truth? Redefining success isn't about lowering the bar as much as it's about moving it. You start valuing peace as much as productivity. You measure your days not by how much you squeezed in, but by how much you savoured.

And perhaps the greatest success of all? Realising you no longer need to prove anything. You did your part. You earned your stripes. Now you get to choose what success looks like, whether it's a perfect golf swing, a well-cooked meal, or simply watching the sunset without glancing at your phone.

So yes, success looks different in retirement. And honestly? That's the best promotion you'll ever get.

Timestamp #76: Starting a Journal (Or a Blog!)

For years, your life was documented in meeting minutes, performance reviews, and emails with subject lines like *"Re: Re: Final (v4.3)."* Retirement, for the first time, gives you the freedom to write... for yourself.

Some people start a journal. Others launch a blog. Either way, it begins the same: a blank page staring back at you. At first, you freeze. No agenda, no template, no "key takeaways." Just space. And oddly, that's terrifying.

Your first attempt. One retiree I know opened his journal and wrote: *"Day 1: Woke up. Had tea. Wondering why I'm writing this."* Another spent an hour debating fonts. I myself once typed out three pages of profound thoughts... only to realise I hadn't saved the file. Lesson learnt: Ctrl+S is as important in retirement as it was in corporate life.

But the magic is in what happens next. Slowly, your words become more natural. You jot down funny moments like trying yoga and discovering muscles you didn't know existed. You capture small joys: the way the morning light falls on your balcony, or how good a simple home-cooked meal tastes when you're not eating it between calls.

If you start a blog (or LinkedIn posts), it gets even better. Suddenly, you're sharing stories with strangers who nod along because they're living the same transition. One person writes back, "This is exactly how I felt!" and you realise: your words matter, even without a corporate memo attached.

Journaling (or blogging) isn't about being profound. It's about reflection. It's a way of reminding yourself that your days *do* have shape, meaning, and memories worth noting. And the act of writing itself becomes its own kind of therapy.

So don't worry about grammar, or whether it sounds "important." Just write. Scribble on paper, type into Word, or even dictate into your phone. Because one day, you'll look back at those pages and smile at the stories you told, the worries you laughed at, the small wins that made retirement uniquely yours.

And who knows? Maybe your grandchildren will find it one day and say, "Wow, grandpa blogged before it was cool again."

Timestamp #77: Mindfulness: Not as a Trend, But a Necessity

During work life, mindfulness was a buzzword sprinkled into wellness workshops. You'd roll your eyes, grab the free stress ball, and rush back to your overflowing inbox. Who had time to "be present" when there were deadlines breathing down your neck?

The script flips now. Suddenly, you have all the time in the world and that's exactly why mindfulness becomes necessary. Without it, time slips by unnoticed. Days blur into weeks, weeks into months, and before you know it, you've binge-watched three seasons of a show you don't even like.

At first, mindfulness feels awkward. You sit with your tea, trying to "be present," only to realise you're mentally drafting a grocery list. Or you attempt deep breathing, only to discover your dog thinks it's playtime. I once tried meditating on the balcony and ended up timing how often the neighbour's pressure cooker whistled. So much for inner peace.

But slowly, you get it. Mindfulness isn't about sitting cross-legged on a mat chanting mantras (though you can, if that's your style). It's about noticing. The warmth of the sun on your face during a morning walk. The taste of tea when you actually sip it slowly instead of gulping between emails. The way your spouse tells the same story, and how it still makes you laugh.

You no longer have the distractions of work to hide behind. You actually notice the squeaky fan, the uneven tile, the neighbour's overly dramatic WhatsApp forwards. At first, it's irritating. Then, strangely enough, it becomes grounding.

The deeper truth: Mindfulness isn't a luxury anymore. It's survival. It keeps you from spiralling into boredom or restlessness. It reminds you that life isn't just about big goals but about the tiny, ordinary moments that make up your days.

So, no, mindfulness isn't a corporate fad anymore. It's not a trend to tick off a list. It's the art of actually living the time you've been given. And in retirement, that might just be the most important skill of all.

Timestamp #78: Digital Detox in Retirement

Technology once felt like proof you were still relevant. Back-to-back calls, late-night emails, calendar invites that multiplied like rabbits, you wore them like badges. Retirement rips away that excuse, and suddenly you have to ask: do I even want to live like that?

At first, the silence feels alien. No red notification bubbles nagging you. No "quick connects" at 8 a.m. Your hand twitches toward the phone out of habit, only to discover… no one's chasing you. WhatsApp groups are filled with recycled jokes, LinkedIn celebrates work anniversaries you don't care about, and emails mostly say "unsubscribe."

That's when the detox begins. You leave the phone in another room for an hour. Then two. Then, courageously over an entire afternoon. You walk without earbuds. You nap without alarms. You eat without scrolling. Instead of FOMO, you start feeling JOMO: the joy of missing out.

Of course, there are relapses. You doomscroll golf reels till midnight and wake up groggy. But the difference is, now you notice the cost. You're no longer enslaved; you're choosing.

A digital detox in retirement isn't about abandoning technology. It's about reclaiming your attention. For decades, your time belonged to everyone else. Now, gloriously, it belongs to you.

Timestamp #79: Understanding Loneliness Without Shame

No one admits it out loud, but retirement can feel lonely. After decades of constant noise, of phones ringing, colleagues popping in, meetings filling your calendar, the silence can feel deafening. One day you're juggling 50 conversations. Next, you're wondering if the courier guy is your new best friend.

At first, you dismiss it. *"I'm not lonely, I'm just… resting."* But then you catch yourself checking WhatsApp a little too often, or talking back to the TV anchors, or dragging out small errands just to exchange pleasantries with the grocer. Loneliness sneaks in quietly, wearing disguises.

You make little adjustments. I once found myself giving full TED Talks to the house plants. Another retiree confessed he talks to Alexa just to hear a human voice, though Alexa calling him "Sorry, I didn't get that" probably didn't help his confidence.

The truth is that loneliness isn't a weakness. It's a signal. It's your mind saying, *"I miss connection."* And acknowledging that is far healthier than pretending everything's fine. You're not broken. You're just adjusting to a new rhythm where relationships aren't built-in anymore, they need to be chosen, nurtured, sometimes even scheduled.

The emotional shift happens when you stop shaming yourself for it. Instead of asking, *"Why am I lonely?"* you start asking, *"What can I do with this space?"* You call an old friend. You join a walking group. You finally say yes to that community class. And slowly, you fill the silence not with noise, but with people who genuinely matter.

And the unexpected upside: in retirement, connections become more authentic. You're no longer "networking." You're just showing up as yourself, no agenda. Some friendships fade, others blossom, but each one feels lighter, more real.

So yes, loneliness happens. But it's nothing to hide. It's simply part of the transition, like learning to sleep without alarms or figuring out how to use Zoom without a secretary. And once you face it without shame, you discover something important: solitude can be a burden, or it can be a doorway. The choice is yours.

Timestamp #80: Reclaiming Curiosity

When you were working, curiosity had boundaries. You googled things like *"market trends 2025"* or *"compliance updates"*, hardly thrilling. If you wanted to learn pottery or astrophysics, it was usually shoved aside with, *"Maybe someday."* Retirement, finally, is someday.

At first, it felt odd. You've spent decades being the expert in the room, and suddenly you're the wide-eyed beginner. I remember signing up for a speed walking group and realising I was the only one struggling while the 25-year-olds jogged ahead. My big achievement that day? Not pulling a muscle. But I came home smiling because I had learned something new (like how not to trust Google Maps on trails).

The joy of curiosity is that it doesn't care about outcomes. Try painting and the tree may look like broccoli, but who cares? Pick up cycling again and you might wobble like a circus act, but the wind on your face makes you feel ten years younger. Curiosity is permission to play without worrying about KPIs.

You notice how small things delight you now. YouTube rabbit holes lead you to learning how to bake sourdough or understanding why penguins mate for life. You ask questions you'd never dare in a boardroom: *"Why is the sky sometimes pink?"* or *"Can I really grow tomatoes on my balcony?"* Spoiler: yes, but the pigeons may file a counterclaim.

Emotionally, curiosity is more than entertainment. It's renewal. It keeps you from shrinking into the familiar and reminds you that life still has surprises tucked away. It helps you see yourself not as "done," but as evolving.

And maybe the best part? Curiosity connects. You meet others equally clueless and equally excited, and suddenly you're part of a new tribe, bonded not by job titles, but by shared wonder.

So reclaim curiosity shamelessly. Ask the silly questions. Try the odd classes. Let yourself be a beginner again. Because retirement isn't the end of learning, it's the first time in decades you can learn purely for the joy of it.

Phase 9

Rebuilding With Intention

The deliberate second innings starts

What is Phase 9?

Up to now, much of retirement has been discovery: testing rhythms, recalibrating health, redefining friendships, and gently untangling identity from old titles. But there comes a moment when drifting no longer feels enough. You've sampled, dabbled, adjusted. Now, you want to choose. This phase is about moving from *experimentation* to *intention*.

Rebuilding with intent doesn't mean filling your days with "shoulds" again. It means asking: *What do I want more of, less of, and why?* It's designing a week that reflects not just curiosity but commitment. Maybe you choose one project to nurture, one community to anchor in, one practice to deepen. The aim isn't scale, but continuity and something you can sustain and grow into.

Expect some pruning here: saying no to activities that drain, to social obligations that don't nourish, to "busywork" that sneaks back in. The joy is that you say no not from guilt, but from clarity.

The goal of this phase is **integration with intention**: shaping your second act deliberately, not accidentally.

When your diary stops looking like a random patchwork and starts resembling a life you're proud to live, you know you've begun rebuilding, not around loss, but around choice.

Timestamp #81: Building a Routine You Actually Enjoy

For decades, your routine was dictated by someone else. Retirement hands you the keys to your own calendar and for the first time, you get to decide what "a good day" looks like.

At first, freedom feels glorious. You wake up without alarms, linger over tea, maybe even scroll the news without guilt. But soon, the absence of structure starts to itch. Days stretch like chewing gum. You forget if it's Tuesday or Sunday. And then one morning, you catch yourself watching a rerun of a show you didn't even like the first time. That's when you realise: you need a routine.

But here's the twist and this one can actually be fun. Instead of "status updates," you schedule a morning walk. Instead of "town halls," you pencil in coffee with friends. Your calendar evolves from being a battlefield to a playground. One retiree I know blocked off afternoons as "nap slots" and defended them fiercely, like boardroom appointments. Honestly, I admire the commitment.

Then there are the small negotiations. You promise yourself you'll meditate, but the couch lures you into Netflix. You vow to swim daily, but the pool looks cold, so you compromise with staring at it. Retirement routines are less about discipline and more about rhythm, about finding what makes you look forward to the next day.

A routine becomes less about filling time and more about shaping life. It creates anchors, small rituals that bring joy and stability. A morning walk, an afternoon read, an evening chat with a friend. None of it looks impressive on LinkedIn, but all of it makes your days richer.

And unlike your work calendar, this one doesn't need colour codes, version numbers, or assistants to manage. It's just yours, simple, flexible, human.

So yes, build a routine. But this time, make it one you actually enjoy. Because after all those years of living to someone else's schedule, you've earned the right to design your own. And if that includes a nap at 3 PM? Call it "strategic recovery."

Timestamp #82: Joining a Community That Aligns With Your Values

Work gives you a ready-made community. Whether you liked your colleagues or not, they were always there, the cafeteria chats, the meeting banter, even the ritual grumbling about work policies. Retirement, though, strips that away. Suddenly, you're on your own. Unless you build something new.

That's where communities come in. Not the kind you were "voluntold" to join at work (remember those team-building sessions?), but the ones you *choose*. It could be a book club, a hiking group, a volunteering circle, or even the WhatsApp gang of morning walkers in your neighbourhood.

The first time you join, it feels awkward. You're the new kid again, except this time with grey hair and bifocals. I once joined a cycling group and discovered everyone else wore Lycra and carried energy gels, while I was just proud my tyres weren't flat. Another retiree I know walked into a photography club only to be asked, "So, are you Canon or Nikon?" He muttered, "Phone," and got a pitying look.

But it's not about skill. It's about shared values. You realise quickly that communities built on common interests feel lighter, friendlier, and more genuine than the politics-heavy groups from office days. No one cares about your designation. They care about whether you'll show up for the next trek, or if you'll bring snacks to the next meeting.

It really shows how liberating it makes you feel. You can actually say no now. No pressure to join the "core committee" unless you really want to. No 11 PM crisis calls. Just people who want to be there, including you.

Communities keep you connected. They give shape to your weeks, energy to your days, and belonging to your new identity. They remind you that retirement isn't about retreating from people but it's about choosing the right people to spend your time with.

So go ahead, join that club, that group, that circle. And if they ask you to bring snacks, bring the good ones. Trust me, that's the fastest way to be accepted.

Timestamp #83: Redefining Productivity

For decades, productivity was your religion. Meetings attended, slides created, miles flown, emails answered at 11:59 p.m. All proof that you were useful, important, necessary. A day without output felt like theft.

Then retirement arrives, and the scoreboard vanishes. No calendar pings, no boss to copy, no "deliverables" that could justify your existence. At first, it feels like drifting. You stand in the kitchen at 10 a.m., clutching your coffee, wondering if brushing your teeth counts as an achievement.

So you try to replicate the old system. You make lists. Colour-coded, prioritised, time-blocked. And within a week, you're laughing at yourself because the list includes items like "buy onions" and "charge phone." By Friday, you award yourself a gold star for successfully updating Netflix.

Slowly, you realise something radical: productivity in retirement isn't about volume. It's about meaning. It's less "How much did I get done?" and more "What actually mattered today?" Fixing the leaky tap, helping your neighbour with groceries, finally finishing that book you abandoned in 2007, all of these count.

One retired friend put it beautifully: "If I go to bed having done one thing useful, one thing joyful, and one thing restful, that's a productive day." That formula sticks. You start measuring output not by spreadsheets but by balance.

The paradox? You often end up doing more but it feels lighter. Without the performance pressure, chores become meditations, hobbies become projects, and naps become legitimate investments in energy.

So when someone asks, "How do you keep busy?" you smile. Because retirement has taught you that being busy is overrated. You don't need a packed calendar to feel alive. You just need a day shaped by usefulness, joy, and rest.

Redefining productivity doesn't mean you've stopped achieving. It means you've finally stopped confusing activity with life

Timestamp #84: Volunteering Surprises

You sign up thinking you'll "give back." Two hours of your time, some wisdom, maybe a pat on the back for being noble. Reality, however, is a prankster.

Day one at the NGO, you expect a warm speech. Instead, someone hands you a broom. Or pairs you with a teenager who explains coding like you're the fossil exhibit at the museum. Retirement humility lesson #1: titles don't mop floors or debug programs.

And yet, this is where the magic lies. You help paint a classroom wall and realise how satisfying it is to see visible progress. A child asks why clouds don't fall down and you fumble, Google sheepishly, and return the next week with an answer that lights up their eyes. An old woman insists on stuffing you with samosas as thanks for carrying her shopping bag. You leave fuller than you arrived, in every sense.

The real surprise? You feel energised, not drained. You gave two hours, but received tenfold in perspective. You thought volunteering was charity. It's actually a mirror. It shows you who you are when PowerPoints and job titles no longer shield you. And sometimes, you like that person even better.

Timestamp #85: Picking One Cause to Go Deep On

Retirement gifts you something you never had enough of before: time. The temptation, of course, is to scatter it everywhere with a little volunteering here, a little committee work there, a dozen "maybe I'll help" promises that leave you busier than your old job. That's when you realise the real challenge isn't finding something to do. It's choosing where to go deep.

At first, it feels impossible. There are so many worthy causes: education, the environment, healthcare, animal welfare, sports, community development. Every appeal tugs at you. And then, of course, there's your family's input: *"Why don't you teach? Why don't you mentor? Why don't you finally start that NGO we've been talking about since 2003?"*

A friend of mine tried volunteering at a school but was politely told by a ten-year-old, "Sir, we already know how to use Google." Another retired executive signed up to clean beaches, only to realise he hated sand in his shoes. I myself once sat in on an NGO board meeting that made corporate strategy sessions look like kindergarten playtime. Lesson learnt: passion is key.

When you do pick one cause, though, it changes everything. Suddenly, your days have purpose again, not the kind tied to targets and revenue, but the kind tied to meaning. You're not just filling hours. You're investing energy into something that outlasts you. And strangely enough, going deep makes you feel lighter. You're no longer stretched thin. You're focused.

Emotionally, it's also healing. Decades of career can leave you asking, *"What did it all add up to?"* Dedicating yourself to one cause, whether it's mentoring young professionals, planting trees, or supporting cancer survivors helps you rewrite that answer. It gives your retirement not just leisure, but legacy.

So, yes, taste-test the options. Try a few things, stumble, laugh, recalibrate. But when you find that one cause that pulls at your heart and makes you forget to check your watch, dive in. That's when retirement stops being just freedom and starts becoming fulfillment.

Timestamp #86: A Side Hustle? Or a Passion Outlet?

One of the first questions people ask you after retirement, right after "So what do you do all day?" is: *"Have you thought of starting something?"* And what they really mean is: *"Are you going to make money again, or are you just painting sunsets?"*

At first, the idea of a side hustle feels thrilling. You imagine yourself launching a boutique consultancy, teaching online courses, maybe even selling pickles (hey, why not?). The spreadsheets in your head start calculating potential income streams before you've even bought the jars.

But then reality winks. Do you really want another round of client calls, invoices, deadlines, and GST filings? Retirement was supposed to liberate you from that, wasn't it? That's where the distinction comes in: hustle versus outlet. One is about income. The other is about joy.

Something arrives mid-experiment. A retired banker I know tried selling his paintings. He made exactly one sale, to his daughter, who hung it out of pity. Another friend started a "consulting" gig that paid less than his old cab allowance but still managed to generate more stress than his last promotion. And me? Let's just say I briefly flirted with the idea of a podcast, until I realised, I sound like a sleepy radio announcer.

The emotional clarity comes when you stop chasing validation and start chasing joy. A passion outlet doesn't have to pay. It just has to light you up. Writing a blog. Coaching a junior for free. Cycling every morning and boring your friends with the details. If it gives you energy instead of draining it, that's the win.

And if, by chance, it earns you a little income? That's gravy. But the main dish is freedom. Freedom to choose projects because you *want* to, not because you *have* to. Freedom to say no without guilt. Freedom to play without attaching ROI.

So yes, explore the hustle if you must. But don't underestimate the power of a passion outlet. After all, the point of retirement isn't to build another business plan. It's to finally give yourself permission to live without one.

Timestamp #87: Making Peace with Being a Beginner Again

Retirement has a funny way of putting you back at square one. After decades of being the "expert in the room," you suddenly find yourself fumbling like a rookie. Whether it's figuring out how to change the TV settings without calling your kids, or learning yoga poses that make you look like a pretzel in distress, you're back in beginner territory.

At first, it bruises the ego. You were once the go-to person for strategy decks, negotiations, and big decisions. Now, you can't figure out why your new hiking boots have more straps than a fighter jet cockpit. The temptation is to grumble: *"I used to run a team of 500, surely I can handle a bicycle helmet."* Spoiler: not always.

Everyone stumbles at the start. I know a retired colleague who joined a painting class and accidentally glued his canvas to the desk. Another proudly told me she "mastered" Zoom only to discover she'd been on mute for half the session. The beauty is, these mistakes no longer carry consequences. No one's firing you for bad downward dog form. No goal is tied to your sourdough starter collapsing.

Emotionally, embracing beginner status is liberating. It teaches humility, the kind that reminds you life is bigger than titles. It also teaches patience, because progress is slow but deeply rewarding. Most importantly, it teaches play. Beginners laugh more, experiment more, and take themselves less seriously. After all, the stakes are low now. No quarterly report depends on you finally learning Spanish.

The secret is to reframe it. Being a beginner isn't a step back, instead it's a step into freedom. You get to try things purely for curiosity's sake, to learn without pressure, to fail without shame. And with each attempt, you not only pick up a skill but also reclaim a sense of wonder you thought you'd left behind years ago.

So yes, make peace with being a beginner again. Trip, stumble, laugh, repeat. Because in retirement, being new at something doesn't mean you're starting over. It means you're still growing and that's the best kind of progress.

Timestamp #88: Generational Mirror

Nothing jolts you into reflection like watching your children or younger colleagues live the exact life you once did.

You see them stumbling out the door with half-eaten toast, eyes glazed from late-night slides. You hear them moaning about office politics, insane deadlines, and the promotion that always feels just out of reach. You sip your tea and think, "That was me, wasn't it?"

At first, you want to intervene. To shortcut their pain, to preach, to save them years of angst. But you've already seen the eye-roll forming when you start with, "In my day..." So you stop. You listen instead. Sometimes you sneak in a gentle, "Remember to sleep," but mostly, you let them run their race.

And then the mirror flips. Their grind makes you question your own: why did you run so fast, miss so much? But it also brings relief: you're past that stage, free of the treadmill.

The generational mirror isn't about judgement. It's perspective. It softens you. You see their stress and feel compassion, not superiority. You look at your calmer mornings and feel gratitude, not guilt.

Their chaos becomes your reminder: you've escaped. And your calm becomes their hope: this grind doesn't last forever.

Timestamp #89: Creating a New Identity Card

For decades, your identity fit neatly on a little rectangle: *Name, Title, Company.* Hand it over at conferences and watch doors open. That small piece of plastic wasn't just an introduction, it was shorthand for credibility, status, belonging.

And then one day, it expires. You're no longer *Managing Director, VP,* or *Head of Something-Something.* You're just… you. Which sounds simple until someone at a party asks, *"So, what do you do?"* and you're tempted to reply, *"Mostly afternoon naps and experimenting with green tea flavours."*

A retired friend of mine had cards printed that said: *"Full-time Grandfather. Part-time Golfer. Occasional Consultant."* Another simply went with: *"Professional Human Being."* I once joked about putting *"Expert at Avoiding Meetings"* under my name, honestly, not a bad branding strategy.

But behind the jokes is a real emotional shift. Retirement forces you to rethink identity. If you're not your title, who are you? A mentor? A traveller? An artist-in-progress? A learner? The answers aren't immediate, and that's okay. The card doesn't need to be printed overnight.

The trick is to see this not as a loss but as a chance. That blank space where your old designation used to be? That's freedom. It means you get to define yourself on your own terms. Not by hierarchy. Not by what HR put in a box. But what matters to you now.

Maybe you don't even need a physical card anymore. Maybe your introductions can be stories instead of labels. "I'm exploring cycling again." "I mentor startups when they'll have me." "I'm learning how not to burn dal." Each answer is honest, human, and far more interesting than *"Senior Vice President of XYZ."*

So yes, create your new identity card. Make it funny, make it personal, make it a reminder that you're more than a title. Because retirement doesn't erase who you were, it just gives you the chance to show who you've always been, beyond the font size on a business card.

Timestamp #90: Feeling Whole Without a Work Role

For most of your life, work wasn't just something you *did*, it was who you *were*. Introductions came with job titles attached, self-worth was tied to performance, and even your family sometimes described you as, *"Oh, he's the banker,"* or *"She's the HR head."* Then retirement arrives, and the label falls off. What's left? Just you.

At first, it feels disorienting. You see younger professionals charging ahead and think, *"Shouldn't I be in that race too?"* You miss the adrenaline of deadlines and, oddly, even the grumbling about them.

But then you begin to realise you're not less whole without work. You're simply whole in a different way. Work fills certain parts of your identity as the provider, leader, problem-solver. Retirement gives you the chance to rediscover the others, friend, spouse, parent, learner, dreamer.

The emotional core is this: you don't need a role to validate your worth. You've already earned your stripes. Now, you get to live without constantly proving yourself. You get to choose activities not because they look impressive on LinkedIn but because they make you feel alive.

For one retiree, that meant gardening. For another, it was mentoring. For me, it was rediscovering how much fun it is to lose badly at golf but laugh harder than I ever did in a boardroom. Each small choice adds up to wholeness.

So yes, the work role is gone. But you? You're still here to complete, curious, maybe a little more wrinkled, but far less rushed. And isn't that the point? To feel whole not because of what you do, but because of who you are when the titles fall away.

Phase 10

The First Year Circle

Reflection, Integration, and Legacy

What is Phase 10?

This phase closes the loop. You're not who you were on Day 1 and that's the point. Conduct a gentle year-end review across four quadrants: Body, Mind, People, Purpose.

What surprised you? What quietly saved you? What can you release? Celebrate tiny, consistent wins; they built this new life.

Mourn what needed mourning; roles, routines, certain friendships and thank them for their season. Capture five "keepers" for next year (habits, relationships, projects) and three experiments to try.

Consider one legacy thread: something you'll build slowly over years (a course, a community circle, a body of writing, a garden).

Design next year's week on one page; leave margin for serendipity. Most of all, update your story: not "retired from," but "rewired for."

The goal of Phase 10 is integration. When your calendar, energy, and relationships broadly rhyme with your values and you hold them all lightly, you're not finishing; you're beginning again, on purpose.

Timestamp #91: Revisiting Your Retirement Letter

When you first wrote your retirement letter, it probably went through more drafts than a corporate strategy deck. Long, short, formal, funny, remember version 47 finally. made it to the outbox. At the time, it felt final, like closing the cover on a well-worn book.

But a year later, you find yourself pulling it out again. Not to edit this time, but to read it with fresh eyes. And suddenly, it feels less like an ending and more like a time capsule. You see the gratitude you expressed, the jokes you slipped in, the careful diplomacy in thanking even the boss who once drove you mad.

You wrote about spending "more time on hobbies", conveniently forgetting you hadn't touched a paintbrush in thirty years. You promised to "keep in touch," yet half the contacts on that farewell thread haven't messaged once. One retiree told me his letter included the line, *"I'll finally improve my golf handicap."* Twelve months later, he admitted, *"It's actually worse."*

But alongside all the fun is something more tender. You realise how much you meant every word of gratitude. You also realise how much you've grown since then. Retirement has reshaped your identity, your priorities, your pace. The letter reminds you of who you were at the edge of that transition, hopeful, nervous, maybe a little dramatic and lets you measure how far you've come.

Revisiting your retirement letter isn't about nostalgia. It's about integration. It connects the professional "you" of yesterday with the evolving "you" of today. It says, *"Yes, that chapter is closed. But it didn't erase you. It carried you forward."*

Some people print their letter and frame it. Others keep it buried in old files. I think the best thing you can do is read it once in a while, not as a farewell, but as a reminder. A reminder that endings can be beautiful, and that beginnings often wear the same clothes.

So go ahead, open that file again. And if you find typos? Leave them. Even imperfection has its place in a good goodbye.

Timestamp #92: Lessons From a Year Without Deadlines

The clock still ticks, but suddenly, it doesn't boss you around. A year into this new rhythm, I've learned three lessons, each from moments that made me smile, stumble, and reflect.

Lesson 1: Freedom is confusing at first.

In my first month, I made the rookie mistake of setting myself a "retirement schedule." Walk at 7. Read at 9. Nap at 2. By week two, my to-do list looked suspiciously like a project plan, complete with sub-tasks and checkboxes. One afternoon, I actually wrote *"Relax from 4 PM to 5 PM."* At 4:03, I was stressed that I wasn't relaxing efficiently. That's when it hit me: I'd carried my corporate habits into my freedom. The first real task of retirement? Unlearning urgency.

Lesson 2: Time expands when you stop chasing it.

A friend decided to clean his garage "by 3 PM." At 2:59, he was frantically dusting shelves, until he paused, laughed, and said, "Who am I trying to impress? The broom?" He finished by sunset, humming, happy, unbothered. Watching him made me realise how nice it feels to *not* measure progress by the clock. These days, I cook without timers, walk without step counts, and write without caring if it's publishable. Turns out, life tastes better when it's slow-cooked.

Lesson 3: What matters now isn't the deadline, but the direction.

In my corporate years, my worth was tied to speed and delivery. In retirement, I ask different questions: *What feels meaningful today? Who do I want to spend time with?* The answers rarely come fast but they come honestly. One morning, I spent three unplanned hours helping a friend fix his old music system. No agenda, no urgency. Just conversation, tinkering, and laughter. It reminded me that being useful doesn't always need to be scheduled.

So yes, deadlines once made me productive. Their absence has made me intentional. These days, I no longer measure my life by what I've finished on time but by what I've had the time to truly finish.

Timestamp #93: The Rituals That Replaced Work

Workdays were stitched together with rituals. The morning coffee in the cafeteria. The 11 AM "quick check-in" that was never quick. The Friday evening exhales over snacks (and maybe a drink) before heading home. These tiny anchors gave shape to your days, even if you didn't notice at the time.

Retirement pulls those anchors out. Suddenly, no one is expecting you at 11 AM. No more townhalls, no more weekly status rituals. At first, it feels like freedom. Then, it feels like drift. What fills the gaps?

That's when new rituals sneak in. A morning walk where you wave at the same group of regulars, the retired army officer, the enthusiastic dog walker, the auntie with unmatched stamina. A leisurely tea on the balcony, watching sunlight shift across the floor. An afternoon swim. Even the silly WhatsApp forwards become part of the rhythm.

New rituals evolve. One retiree I know has a "chai gang" that meets every evening at exactly 5 PM, rain or shine. Another takes his car out daily, not because he needs to, but because the parking attendant expects him now. Personally, I discovered the guilty joy of organising my bookshelf over and over again, at least books don't demand status updates.

The emotional core is this: rituals aren't trivial. They're what keep life steady, meaningful, and surprisingly comforting. You don't miss the spreadsheets; you miss the small exchanges that framed your day. And when you create new rituals, you're not just filling time but you're creating a new structure that belongs entirely to you.

The trick is to make them light, enjoyable, and flexible. No corporate rigidity required. A daily walk can be skipped for rain. A 5 PM chai can turn into a 5:30 catch-up with a friend. The point isn't precision. The point is rhythm.

So yes, retirement takes away the old rituals. But it also hands you the gift of creating new ones, ones that don't drain you, don't come with reviews, and don't need to be booked on Outlook. Just small, steady reminders that life still has a beat, and you get to choose the tune.

Timestamp #94: The Expanded Social Circle

One of the quiet surprises of retirement is how your social circle doesn't shrink but it shapeshifts. For years, your world revolved around colleagues, clients, and cafeteria companions. You didn't choose your tribe; the firm did it for you. The colleague who sat next to you became your lunch buddy. The teammate who survived those midnight calls with you became your confidant. The "coffee break gang" became your de facto social club.

Then retirement arrives. You realise that some friendships were built on proximity, not permanence. Shared calendars, not shared lives. But give it time and the social tide doesn't recede; it returns in a new shape.

Because of the beauty of this phase? You start meeting people you'd never have encountered in your working life. The early-morning walkers who greet you with "same time tomorrow?" The neighbour who finally has more than three seconds to chat. The barista who knows your order and your mood better than your ex-assistant ever did.

It's a whole new ecosystem, one not built around deadlines, but daylight. Conversations are lighter, curiosity runs deeper, and everyone's unhurried enough to listen. I met a retired naval officer who now leads bird-watching walks. Another friend joined a cycling group and found himself bonding with twenty-somethings who now call him "uncle," but with genuine affection. These new friendships feel refreshing, less competitive, more collaborative, fuelled by shared discovery rather than shared stress.

Of course, a few old connections remain, and those become even more special. The ex-colleague who still checks in, the junior who calls for advice, the friend who remembers your birthday without a LinkedIn reminder. They form the steady roots under all the new growth.

Retirement doesn't make you lonely. It just makes you selective. It prunes the noise and leaves you with voices that matter. And in the process, your social circle doesn't shrink, it expands, one unexpected, energising connection at a time.

Timestamp #95: The Trip You Finally Took for Yourself

For years, travel was a negotiation between school holidays, family itineraries, business trips with "a quick sightseeing detour" if the client cancelled. There was always someone else's calendar to check. Then retirement happened, and for the first time, I booked a trip that was purely, unapologetically mine: a trek to Everest Base Camp.

Just a backpack, a trail, and an altitude chart that looked mildly terrifying.

The first shock hit at the airport, no laptop in my bag, no "Out of Office" reply to set, no guilt about unread emails. My phone went from lifeline to paperweight the higher we climbed. By Day 3, the Wi-Fi stopped working, and so did my inner need to check for messages. Somewhere between Namche Bazaar and Tengboche, I realised that no one was waiting for a reply, and the world was doing just fine without me.

The trek itself was a masterclass in humility. Every step above 10,000 feet reminded me that lungs have opinions. The younger trekkers floated past with Bluetooth playlists and GoPros, while I developed a deep, personal bond with my walking stick. There were moments of laughter like the day I proudly ordered "hot lemon tea" and accidentally received a bowl of lemon soup and moments of silence so pure that even my thoughts whispered.

At night, in the mountain lodges, conversation replaced connectivity. Stories were swapped over soup instead of screens. Nobody asked, "What do you do?" The only relevant question was, "How are you holding up?"

By the time I reached Base Camp, winds cutting across my face, prayer flags fluttering, Everest gleaming in the distance, something inside me had shifted. It wasn't about conquering anything. It was about arriving, finally, somewhere unmeasured.

That trek wasn't an escape from the world; it was a return to myself. No phones, no pings, no inbox. Just the rhythm of boots on stone and the sound of your own breath.

Retirement didn't take me away from purpose. It gave me a new one, to climb slowly, breathe deeply, and live without deadlines. And honestly, the view from there beats any corner office.

Timestamp #96: Teaching, My New Obsession

One of the unexpected perks of retirement? People suddenly think you're wise. Former colleagues call for "quick advice," students message on LinkedIn, and occasionally even my kids pause their scrolling to ask, "Dad, how do you handle office politics?"

At first, I treated these as casual chats. But old habits die hard and five minutes in, I'd unconsciously stand up, find a whiteboard, and start drawing 2x2 matrices. The corporate muscle memory kicked in with frameworks, bullet points, key takeaways. It wasn't long before I realised: I hadn't retired from teaching; I'd just been promoted to a new audience.

That's how the classroom found me again. What began as a guest lecture turned into a passion. Now, I teach regularly at business schools, wide-eyed undergraduates, sharp MBAs, sometimes even mid-career executives who think they've seen it all (until the case study hits).

The energy in those rooms is addictive. It's nothing like the conference calls of old. These students challenge, question, laugh, sometimes at me, sometimes with me and remind me that learning is a two-way street. The joy isn't in "delivering content." It's in watching curiosity spark.

I've learned to swap jargon for jokes. To replace PowerPoint slides with personal stories. The day I shared how a multi-million-dollar hiring plan went sideways because of one unchecked assumption, they listened, gasped, laughed, and learned more than any textbook could have taught them.

And of course, the occasional ego-check keeps things balanced. Like when I once delivered a dramatic build-up to a "career-defining insight," only for a student to raise her hand and ask, "Sir, are you on Instagram? I think I saw that quote there." Touché.

Teaching, I've realised, isn't about preaching. It's not about telling people *what* to do, but showing them *why it matters.* The corporate years gave me the lessons; the classroom gives them meaning.

Every time I step into that lecture hall, marker in hand, I feel the same excitement I once did before a big client pitch, except now, the goal isn't to close a deal, it's to open a mind.

So yes, retirement took me out of the boardroom. But it handed me something far more rewarding, a front-row seat to the next generation, and the sheer joy of passing the mic, not holding it.

Timestamp #97: A day Well Lived

Some days don't make it to your résumé, but they're the ones that truly count.

The day starts early, not because an alarm told you to, but because your body clock is still convinced you have a morning meeting. Only this time, the meeting is with the sun. A quiet stretch, a lazy read of the headlines, and then golf.

Ah, golf. The sport that teaches patience, humility, and creative vocabulary. The familiar banter begins before the first tee. "Same old swing?" someone jokes. "Only if you promise not to lose the first ball." The course is your new boardroom, lush, silent, dotted with laughter and the occasional curse word disguised as philosophy. The only metrics that matter are fairways hit and coffee consumed.

By mid-morning, you're back in civilization. A quick coffee with an old friend, the kind where the conversation starts mid-sentence because you've known each other for decades. No networking, no agenda, no LinkedIn updates. Just stories, exaggerated for effect, punctuated by laughter. You swap retirement notes, pretend you miss the chaos, and both know you don't.

The afternoon drifts by gently. A book that's been waiting for years finally gets its due. The same chair, the same view, but a different kind of peace. There's no background buzz of email notifications, no guilt about "wasting time." You doze off for a bit, the nap that would've once felt like indulgence now feels like reward.

Evening brings family into the frame. The house smells of dinner, laughter echoes from the kitchen. Someone's telling a story, someone else is arguing about the cricket score. You're not leading, not managing, you are just *there*. Present, grounded, grateful.

No milestones. Just a day that flowed without friction where you hit a few decent shots, shared a few laughs, read a few pages, and ended with the people who matter most.

It's not glamorous. It's not "productive." But it's perfect.

Because in retirement, success is measured not in hours billed or targets met but in days like this, quietly, beautifully, well-lived.

Timestamp #98: Starting Again (New Projects, Not New Jobs)

No one tells you this, but retirement has a funny way of reintroducing you to yourself. Once the titles fade and the inbox goes quiet, there's an itch that doesn't go away, to *build again*, but differently this time.

That's how my new organization was born. Not as a business plan with revenue charts or investor decks, but as a passion project that slowly found its rhythm, to become India's first dedicated *non-financial retirement coaching practice.*

For decades, I'd spent my career helping others grow, teams, talent, leaders, institutions. And yet, when it came to my own transition, I realised how little anyone prepared you for life after work. The conversations were always about money, never about meaning. That gap became my calling.

So I started again. From spreadsheets to soul sheets. From performance reviews to purpose reviews. What began as a few reflective notes and casual conversations over coffee became something much bigger, workshops, tools, and assessments designed to help people rediscover joy, connection, and curiosity in retirement.

I called it Silver Spring because it felt right and a reminder that this phase isn't about fading out, but flowing forward. There's a quiet beauty in helping someone who's standing at the edge of their career realise that the next chapter can be richer, freer, and more *exciting* than ever before.

Has it been easy? Of course not. Building something new after years in structured environments is like switching from an orchestra to a jazz solo. There's no script, no boss, no quarterly review, just instinct and intent. But that's also the thrill.

And the reward? Every time someone finishes a session and says, "I didn't think about retirement this way before," I know Silver Spring isn't just my project. It's my purpose. It gave shape to my own transition and a mirror to everything I'd learned, unlearned, and still discovering.

So yes, I started again. Not with deadlines, but with direction. Not with deliverables, but with kindness.

Silver Spring isn't just something I built. It's something that rebuilt *me*.

Timestamp #99: Who You've Become, A Letter to Your Younger Self

If retirement gives you one luxury, it's perspective. For the first time in decades, you can look back at the long road you've walked, the detours, the shortcuts, the wrong turns, the scenic routes and see how it all added up. Sometimes, the best way to capture that reflection is to write a letter to your younger self.

It begins playfully. *"Dear 25-year-old me, relax about the tie colour. No one cares."* Or, *"Dear 30-year-old me, you don't need to attend every meeting you're invited to. Half of them should've been emails."* The humour softens the memories, letting you laugh at the things that once felt monumental but now look like footnotes.

Then it turns tender. You might write, *"You're going to work harder than you think, but you'll also love more deeply than you imagine. You'll make mistakes that feel crushing in the moment but turn out to be lessons that shape you."* Or, *"You'll lose some people along the way, and that will hurt but it will also teach you to hold the ones who stay even closer."*

The realisation hits: you've become someone your younger self couldn't have fully pictured. Not just a professional with titles and paychecks, but a human with resilience, humour, and scars that tell stories. And while your younger self may have been chasing promotions, your retired self knows the bigger prize was the relationships, the laughter, the everyday rituals that gave life its texture.

One retiree I know ended his letter with: *"You'll be proud of the career, but prouder of the person you become outside it."* That, perhaps, is the point. Work mattered, but it wasn't the whole story.

The emotional gift of this exercise is acceptance. You stop judging the "what ifs" and start appreciating the "what was." You see continuity instead of gaps. And in writing to your younger self, you give your present self the closure and the kindness it deserves.

So go ahead, draft that letter. Make it funny, make it tender, make it yours. Because if retirement teaches you anything, it's that the best conversation you'll ever have is the one between who you were and who you've become.

Timestamp #100: The Quiet Satisfaction of a Life Rewritten

Retirement isn't the grand finale people imagine. There's no confetti cannon, no dramatic curtain drop, no orchestra playing you out. What you get instead is something quieter, mornings that stretch without alarms, days that unfold without agendas, evenings that close without the stress of "what's due tomorrow." At first, it felt odd. Eventually, it feels like satisfaction. The kind that comes not with noise, but with stillness.

The satisfaction isn't about what you've achieved, the titles, the promotions, the deals. Those were important, yes, but they fade into the background quicker than you expect. What lingers is subtler. The way a junior once told you your advice changed her career. The friendships that outlived the office. The rituals like chai breaks, corridor jokes, Friday laughs that carried you through years. That's the real treasure chest you open in retirement.

You thought satisfaction would feel like standing at the top of a mountain, arms wide, dramatic music playing. Instead, it's sipping tea on your balcony, watching sunlight move across the floor, and thinking, *"I'm exactly where I need to be."* It's learning how to finally fix the squeaky door that annoyed everyone for years. It's not glamorous, but it's deeply, almost comically, human.

And then there's the rewriting part. Retirement gives you a pen you didn't know you had. You start to edit old scripts: the story that said you were only valuable if you were busy, the story that tied your worth to a designation, the story that made you feel guilty for resting. Slowly, line by line, you scribble those out. You replace them with something softer, truer. You discover you can be useful without being exhausted, present without being scheduled, proud without being promoted.

You learn to accept yourself not for what you do, but for who you are. That's not an easy transition. Some days, you miss the rush, the chaos, the validation. Other days, you wonder if you're doing retirement "right." But over time, the doubts fade, and a quieter confidence settles in. You realise you don't need to prove anything anymore, not to your boss, not to your colleagues, not even to yourself. You've already done enough.

And that's the satisfaction. Not the fireworks, not the applause, not the speeches. Just the quiet knowledge that you've lived, worked, loved, stumbled, laughed and now, you get to live again, differently, with more presence. A life not finished, but rewritten.

So when you sit back, one year into retirement, and someone asks how it feels, you don't launch into a speech. You smile, maybe sip your tea, and say, "It feels enough. More than enough."

Because in the end, that's the gift of retirement: not perfection, not performance, but peace.

Closing Chapter

From Whisper to Rewire

When I began this journey with you, it started with a whisper. A question so quiet it could easily be ignored: *"Should I retire?"*

It wasn't shouted in boardrooms or scribbled on sticky notes during quarterly reviews. It came in those hushed, private moments when you wondered if there was more to life than another performance cycle, another presentation, another late-night call.

Over the course of these 100 timestamps, we've walked through that whisper's echo, from the early doubts to the bold decision, from farewells to first mornings of freedom, from restless experiments to steady routines.

If you've travelled with me this far, you'll know retirement is not a cliff edge. It's a long, winding transition, sometimes amusing, sometimes unsettling, often unexpectedly liberating. It is less about leaving something behind and more about stepping into a new rhythm of being.

The Arc We Travelled

Looking back, the journey unfolded in distinct chapters.

It began with thought. The first whispers, the calendar glances, the quiet envy of a colleague's farewell. Doubt mixed with anticipation. Retirement seemed both tempting and terrifying.

Then came the decision. Drafting that unsent resignation email. Realising promotions no longer sparkled. Watching yourself fade in meetings, not out of incompetence but because the torch was quietly being passed. There was sadness in the "lasts", the last commute, the last scan of your ID card, the last farewell lunch. But also relief. Each "last" was really a "first" in disguise.

And then the firsts arrived. The first Monday with no alarm. The first Tuesday lunch that wasn't hurried. The first holiday without checking email. These firsts felt exhilarating, sometimes strange, occasionally awkward. You stumbled, you laughed, you improvised.

Slowly, a rhythm emerged. Old hobbies were rediscovered; new skills attempted. Family became the best workout routine. Music sounded sweeter. Sleep became sacred. You found that time, which once raced ahead, now walked beside you.

And finally, perspective. Legacy no longer meant titles or plaques. It meant people, relationships, echoes. Gratitude became a practice, not a platitude. Success stopped being about numbers and started being about mornings, afternoons, and evenings well spent. One year later, you realised retirement wasn't about stepping out. It was about stepping in — into yourself, into life, into rewiring rather than retiring.

Advice for the Road Ahead

Now that we've walked through these 100 reflections, let me leave you with a few distilled lessons. They are not rules. They're reminders, companions for your own journey.

1. Retirement is not a finish line.
   For decades, we're conditioned to see retirement as "the end" of the working chapter. But it's really the beginning of a new book. Think of it less as "retiring from" and more as "retiring to." To hobbies, to family, to projects, to yourself.

2. Give yourself permission to be a beginner.
   Whether it's painting, cooking, or yoga, retirement is your license to start clumsy and laugh through it. You don't need targets for hobbies. Joy doesn't need a performance review.

3. Balance solitude with community.

   Retirement offers silence. Sometimes too much. Cherish it, but don't isolate it. Seek out people, friends, neighbours, classmates, fellow retirees. Human connection is not optional; it's oxygen.

4. Guard your health fiercely.

   Time is your biggest currency, but health is the bank that holds it. Invest in walks, check-ups, stretching, mindful eating. It's not about living longer. It's about living well.

5. Redefine success on your own terms.

   Success used to be tied to promotions and paychecks. Now, success is a day well lived. A nap guilt-free. A laugh with an old friend. A walk where the only deadline is the sunset.

6. Legacy lives in people, not plaques.

   You won't be remembered for quarterly numbers. You will be remembered for kindness, mentorship, humour, presence. Build echoes, not monuments.

7. Learn to say "no" and mean it.

   Work life trained us to say yes. Retirement invites you to be selective. Protect your time. Protect your energy. "No" is not selfish. It's wise.

8. Stay curious.

   The world will move on without you. New technologies, trends, acronyms you don't understand. Don't chase them. But do stay curious. Ask questions. Read widely. Curiosity keeps you alive.

9. Expect wobbles.

   There will be days of doubt, even regret. Days when you miss the camaraderie, the rhythm, the identity. That's normal. It doesn't mean retirement was wrong. It means you're human.

10. Remember: you're rewiring, not retiring.

    The word "retire" suggests retreat, withdrawal. The truth is the opposite. You're rewiring your time, your identity, your relationships. You're not fading out. You're shifting gears.

A Gentle Reminder

If there's one truth retirement teaches us, it's this: time was always the real wealth. We just didn't notice when it was hidden under emails, meetings, and targets. Retirement strips away the noise and hands you time, sometimes awkwardly, sometimes abundantly.

What you do with it is up to you. Some will fill it with travel. Others with gardening. Some will volunteer. Others will nap. There is no right way. There is only your way.

And if you ever feel guilty, for not being "productive," for not "optimising" every minute, just remember this: productivity was for careers. Retirement is for living.

A Closing Thought

One year later, you'll look back, just as I did in Timestamp #100. You'll remember the fear, the hesitation, the sleepless nights. And you'll smile. Because in the end, you'll discover the same thing I did: you weren't retiring. You were rewiring.

So here's my wish for you: may your rewiring be intentional, compassionate, and empowering. May your days be filled with laughter, your nights with rest, and your heart with purpose. May you find joy in the small, courage in the new, and gratitude in the ordinary.

And if anyone asks you what you "do" now that you're retired, just smile and say:

"I do life. On my terms."

The Beginning

If you think retirement is a never-ending vacation filled with golf, grandkids, and guilt-free naps, think again.

In *Brew Your Retirement*, **Rajat Mathur**, former corporate leader turned **Retirement Transition Coach** and Founder of **Silver Spring**, takes a witty, honest, and deeply relatable look at what really happens when the work emails stop but life doesn't.

Through 100 bite-sized reflections, or "timestamps," Rajat captures the small, funny, and often thought-provoking moments that make up the emotional side of retirement: the joy of slow mornings, the unease of unstructured days, the challenge of sharing space (and Wi-Fi) with your equally retired spouse, and that awkward question everyone loves to ask; *"So, what do you do now?"*

Blending self-deprecating humour with quiet insight, he paints a picture of retirement that's as real as it is reassuring. It's not a self-help manual; it's more like having coffee with a friend who's been there, done that, and is still figuring it out, one sip at a time.

This is a **light, engaging, and reflective read** that will make you laugh, nod, and occasionally pause to think, *"That happened to me too."* It gently nudges you to see retirement not as an ending, but as a fascinating transition, one where you can rebuild, rediscover, and redefine what "purpose" means when the business card no longer does the talking.

For those **contemplating retirement**, this book offers a glimpse into what lies ahead, the good, the odd, and the surprisingly liberating. For those **already in it**, it's a comforting reminder that you're not alone on this unpredictable adventure.

And for everyone else, it makes a **perfect gift**, a coffee-table companion for anyone stepping into the "silver zone," equal parts laughter, truth, and gentle perspective.

Because maybe retirement isn't about stopping.

It's just another coffee break, one that finally lasts long enough to savour.

www.ingramcontent.com/pod-product-compliance
Lightning Source LLC
LaVergne TN
LVHW100306210926
848480LV00003B/1034